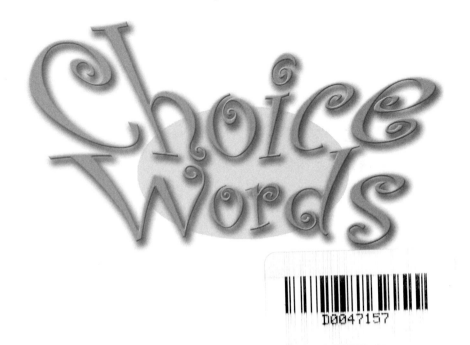

D0047157

PROPERTY OF T.C.S.D. #1
CURRICULUM DEPT.

Sticks and Stones May Break My Bones

"Sticks and stones may break my bones
But words could never hurt me."
And this I knew was surely true
And truth could not desert me.

But now I know it is not so.
I've changed the latter part;
For sticks and stones may break the bones
But words can break the heart.

Sticks and stones may break the bones
But leave the spirit whole,
But simple words can break the heart
Or silence crush the soul.

HERB WARREN

How Our Language Affects Children's Learning

PETER H. JOHNSTON

State University of New York at Albany

Stenhouse Publishers

Portland, Maine

Stenhouse Publishers
www.stenhouse.com

Copyright © 2004 by Peter H. Johnston

Every effort has been made to contact copyright holders and students for permission to reproduce borrowed material. We regret any oversights that may have occurred and will be pleased to rectify them in subsequent reprints of the work.

Credits

Frontispiece: From "Sticks and Stones May Break My Bones" in *Herb's Poems: A Collection* by H. J. Warren. Copyright © 1982 by Friends of H. J. Warren. Reprinted by permission of Archimedes Press, Rockport, Maine.

Pages 49–50: From *How's It Going?* by Carl Anderson. Copyright © 2000 by Carl Anderson. Published by Heinemann, a division of Reed Elsevier, Inc., Portsmouth, NH. All rights reserved. Reprinted by permission.

Adapted excerpts, pp. 225–229, from *Journal of Educational Psychology*, 2001, 93: 223–233. Copyright © 2001 by the American Psychological Association. Adapted with permission.

Library of Congress Cataloging-in-Publication Data
Johnston, Peter H.
    Choice words : how our language affects children's learning / Peter H. Johnston.
        p. cm.
    Includes bibliographical references.
    ISBN 1-57110-389-9 (alk. paper)
    1. Communication in education. 2. Interaction analysis in education. 3. Educational psychology. I. Title.
LB1033.5.J64 2004
370.15'23—dc22   2004042900

Manufactured in the United States of America on acid-free paper
19 18 17 16 15 14   20 19 18 17 16 15

For all my parents—
Betty and Bruce Johnston
Mary and John Miceli (in-law)
Rosalie and Greg Clarke (adopted)—

and for all the wonderful teachers
who have allowed me to learn from them

Contents

Foreword

About twenty-five years ago I noticed that primary-grade teachers often used language differently, depending on whom they were teaching. From recordings of reading instruction, I documented three differences in the ways teachers interacted with more and less successful readers (Allington 1980). They interrupted successful readers less often and waited longer for them to figure words out, and their comments to them focused on making sense rather than on the details of print, on sustaining their efforts rather than on correcting them. They said, "Does that make sense?," "Does that sound right?," and "Let's try that again," rather than, "Sound it out." All their comments to more successful readers suggested that reading was about making sense. Although I knew this was a critical difference, I didn't follow those instructional conversations any further. I don't think I understood that these seemingly small differences were simply the tip of the iceberg when it comes to the importance of the language we use with children day in, day out.

About a decade after that study was published, Peter Johnston and I began a sustained collaborative research partnership. Peter tried over the next decade to help me learn to notice other aspects of teacher instructional talk. Perhaps it was my roots in direct instruction as an instructional model that held me back. I tended to focus on what I dubbed explicitness and thoughtfulness and strategies talk while not noticing the social, moral, and personal aspects of teachers' language. Perhaps, too, it was the relative infrequency of the sorts of talk that Peter describes in this skinny book that made noticing it difficult for me. Sitting day after day in the classrooms of the many superb teachers we studied together, I noticed the strategy talk. I noticed the overwhelmingly positive nature of these teachers' interactions with their students (see also Pressley and his colleagues 2003). I noticed the more conversational nature of the instructional interactions (Allington 2002). I didn't notice most of the things Peter was noticing while observing many of the same classrooms.

It's not that what I noticed was wholly trivial, but that I had no way of thinking about what I saw and heard that would allow me to notice what Peter noticed and to understand what Peter explains in this book. I knew about self-regulation, metacognition, self-efficacy, and a variety of other psychological frames for explaining differences between readers, and even between classrooms. By analogy, I was able to notice that the Florida Gators had sacked the opposing quarterback but was unable to see the crucial breakdown in pass blocking that allowed that to happen. So, even though Peter and I spent a decade working together in these classrooms, reading this book has provided me with new eyes. I will verify the reliability of the observations he details. I heard these teachers say these things. I will testify that his analysis of the talk in these rooms provides the reader with powerful insights into just how forcefully language shapes thinking about reading and writing, and about becoming readers and writers and social beings.

Peter also noticed that others, both teachers and researchers, have attempted to convey the power of the sort of talk that teachers in this book routinely use as they go about their work. He illustrates many of the ideas with talk from other studies. But I think Peter is the first to pull all this together in a format that is engaging and accessible to the broad education audience, and to give every reader new eyes for observing classrooms.

I wish I had written this book. Actually, I wish I'd been able to write it. I am truly grateful for *Choice Words*, and I wish there was a way to ensure that every teacher, teacher educator, school administrator, and researcher would read it. Maybe then our discussions, our lessons, our research, and maybe, our educational policies could move beyond debating what sort of lessons garner higher test scores, and instead, focus on how our lessons develop not just readers and writers, but literate citizens for a democratic society.

RICHARD ALLINGTON

Acknowledgments

This book grew out of a project begun by Michael Pressley and Dick Allington as part of the National Research Center on English Learning and Achievement (CELA). Because my collaborations with Dick go back twenty-three years, my debt to him is particularly extensive. I am also indebted to the codirectors of CELA, Arthur Applebee and Judith Langer, particularly for their leadership and for assembling a wonderful support staff—especially Mary Murphy and Janet Angelis, who have been extraordinarily supportive over the years. Funding for this project was provided through CELA, by the Research and Development Centers Program (Grant No. R305A960005) as administered by the Office of Educational Research and Improvement (now Institute of Education Sciences), U.S. Department of Education. I also owe thanks to the other CELA researchers who were part of the original project: Cathy Collins Block, Gay Ivey, Leslie Morrow, Ruth Wharton-McDonald, Nancy Farnan, Marcie Cox, and Helen Foster James, along with research assistants Kim Boothroyd, Greg Brooks, Melissa Cedeno, John Cronin, Jeni Pollack Day, Susan Leyden, Steven Powers, Jean Veltema, and Haley Woodside-Jiron.

I cannot thank enough the wonderful teachers who let my colleagues and me into their classrooms to document their teaching practice, particularly the ones I observed personally. They taught me so much. Each showed me a different face and voice of the genius of teaching. I hope that this book does some justice to their remarkable daily work.

I have quoted quite a bit of material in this book, and I appreciate the consideration of the publishers who gave me permission to do so: the American Psychological Association, Guilford Press, Heinemann, Stenhouse, and Teachers College Press. I particularly appreciate the permission to reprint the poem by Herb Warren that appears as a frontispiece. If you would like to read more of his wonderful poetry, the book *Herb's Poems* is available only from the Friends of H. J. Warren at Box 399, Camden, Maine 04843.

I have been blessed with a wonderfully supportive group of colleagues at the State University of New York at Albany: Jim Collins, Cheryl Dozier, KaiLonnie Dunsmore, Ginny Goatley, Mark Jury, George Kamberelis, Donna Scanlon, Margi Sheehy, Sean Walmsley, and Rose Marie Weber. Along with Mary Unser and Linda Papa, they sustain my work.

Marie Clay's work on prompting children in Reading Recovery stimulated my thinking about teachers' responses to children's reading—and almost everything else in literacy teaching and learning. Jim Collins and Becky Rogers played an important role in developing my interest in and understanding of teachers' use of language. Becky and, more recently, Paula Costello have helped extend my interest and my thinking through sharing articles and discussions. Conversations with Cheryl Dozier and Barbara Gioia over the years of teaching together have also helped my thinking enormously.

In writing the book I have had helpful feedback and encouragement at various times from Ginny Goatley, Paula Costello, Becky Rogers, Cheryl Dozier, Gay Ivey, Jennifer Gray, and Jamie Conway. Similarly, no footnote can express my appreciation for the feedback and assistance from the wonderful editors at Stenhouse: Brenda Power, Philippa Stratton, and Martha Drury. Remaining inadequacies in the book are my responsibility.

Throughout the writing, I have been sustained, as ever, by my family: Tina, Nicholas, Emily, and Samantha. To them I must apologize for my frequent failures to engage them through the language I know to be most helpful. I hope they forgive this frailty.

The Language of Influence in Teaching

When I was in fourth grade, my teacher turned to me in response to one of my transgressions and said with relish, "By the gods, thou art a scurvy knave. Verily I shall bonce thee on thine evil sconce." An observer might have chuckled and forgotten this brief and trivial event. Its genius is easily missed. My teacher's playful use of language got my attention, stopping the inappropriate behavior, but at the same time it took the edge off the rebuke by making it playful, leaving my dignity intact (showing that he cared), and it showed me how valuable and interesting language can be—valuable enough to play with, powerful enough to change behavior without force. He also showed the possibilities for adopting other voices, drawing language from other sources, while incidentally reminding us of a topic we had studied in social studies. It would be foolish to argue that this single event is the reason I use language as I do in my learning, thinking, teaching, and social life. It would be less foolish, I think, to point to it as an example of a conversational current that left its mark on my social and intellectual being. As with most of the teachers it has been my privilege to study, I doubt that my fourth-grade teacher was aware of the implications of how he used language. He was just good at using it in ways that assisted our learning. Some of us have to think more carefully about the language we use to offer our students the best learning environment we can.

Recently, my colleagues and I had the privilege of studying how successful literacy teachers work their magic in the classroom (Allington and Johnston 2002b). We selected these teachers as successful both because their students did well on conventional literacy tests and because people who were familiar with their work recommended them, aspired to be like them, or wished to have them teach their children. Each was excellent in his or her own way, and each had areas with which he or she struggled, just like the rest of us. I became particularly interested in the powerful and subtle ways these teachers used language, and began to explore its significance. In this book I focus on those things teachers say (and don't say) whose combined effect changes the literate lives of their students. I use examples of apparently ordinary words, phrases, and uses of language that are pivotal in the orchestration of the classroom. I drew my examples initially from the teachers in our study, and I have added examples from the work of other researchers and from my own experience to elaborate certain points.

My initial interest was in how teachers' use of language might explain their students' success in becoming literate, as documented on literacy tests. However, I frequently watched teachers accomplish remarkable things with their students and at the end of the day express guilt about their failure to accomplish some part of the curriculum. This guilt was, in my view, both unfounded and unproductive. It was caused, in part, by the teachers' inability to name all the things they *did* accomplish. Consequently, my second goal with this book is to reduce this guilt by showing the complex learning that teachers produce that is not recognized by tests, policy makers, the general public, and often even by teachers themselves, but that is particularly important.

If we have learned anything from Vygotsky (1978), it is that "children grow into the intellectual life around them" (p. 88). That intellectual life is fundamentally social, and language has a special place in it. Because the intellectual life is social, it is also relational and emotional. To me, the most humbling part of observing accomplished teachers is seeing the subtle ways in which they build emotionally and relationally healthy learning communities—intellectual environments that produce not mere technical competence, but caring, secure, actively literate human beings. Observing these teachers accomplish both goals convinced me that the two achievements are not completely at odds.

Some years ago, I read Mary Rose O'Reilley's *The Peaceable Classroom*. Early in the book she observes, "I had gone off to be a teacher, asking myself from time to time if it might be possible to teach English in such a way that people would stop killing each other" (O'Reilley 1993, p. 30). When I first encountered this confession, I was reminded of my own journey into teaching and filed both under youthful idealism. However, I happened to reread the passage while studying these teachers and realized I had been wrong. It is both realistic and fundamental. In one classroom, I noticed a student return from the library with a book. His teacher looked up and asked if he had found the book he needed for his project. His cheerful answer? "Not yet, but I found one for Richard." In another school, I watched a whole class of fourth graders engage in a deeply philosophical discussion of science and ethics for an hour and a quarter with little input from the teacher. In another, over the course of four months, I watched as a student, who had been classified as emotionally disturbed, was systematically made undisturbed, becoming a "normal" participant in class activities with none of his former outbursts. In the face of relentless testing pressures, these teachers were accomplishing some of what O'Reilley imagined—not without struggle, and not without soliciting the help of the students in their classes.

Exploring the nature of these teachers' skill, I have been particularly influenced by what children have to say. My colleague Rose Marie Weber says that as a graduate student at Cornell she was introduced to some first graders. One of the girls commented that her father was going to be a doctor of philosophy. The teacher observed that Rose was, too. The girl immediately pointed out that Rose couldn't be a doctor of philosophy, that she would have to be a nurse of philosophy. This is even funnier now that Rose is a member of the International Reading Association's Hall of Fame, but beyond the humor is something a little darker. This first grader could not imagine herself becoming a doctor. Doubtless, she also could not imagine her brother becoming a nurse. She didn't just make this up out of nothing. She made it up out of the linguistic—or, more broadly, the discursive—environment in which she was immersed.

Children, in their own ways, teach us about the language of our classrooms. We have to ask what discursive histories have made it possible for them to say what they say. What makes it possible for a student asked, "Who else would like that book?" to respond, "Probably Patrick. . . . He's, he's not the kind of guy who laughs, and he doesn't smile too much. And in this book, he might smile" (Allington and Johnston 2002,

p. 201). Why does another student describe herself thus: "I'm on one of the lowest levels in this class. It really stinks. . . . Most of them [classmates] are above me. . . . I have Peter Williams and he doesn't care if I read with him and he always helps me out and stuff." How come a student in a different class distinguishes herself as a reader with, "I love to read mystery, adventure, suspense, and I like to read books about animals doing everyday things that we do (Johnston, Bennett, and Cronin 2002b, p. 194). . . . Barry likes to read about sports. And Amy likes to read about horses and dolphins. . . . Amanda's reading is very different from mine because hers usually have a happy ending. Mine are like never-ending stories." What classroom conversations lead to a student reporting that, "[recently] I have learned how to pronounce more words. . . . How to read more faster than before. . . . I'd like to learn how to pronounce more words" (Wharton-McDonald, Boothroyd, and Johnston 1999, p. 2)?

Teachers play a critical role in arranging the discursive histories from which these children speak. Talk is the central tool of their trade. With it they mediate children's activity and experience, and help them make sense of learning, literacy, life, and themselves.

An Example

Let me give a slightly more expanded example of what I have in mind. Consider the following transcript from a Reading Recovery lesson (Lyons 1991, p. 209):

Mary: You said, "I will to my friend, the car driver." Does this word look like *will*?
Melissa: No.
Mary: What letters would you expect to see if the word was *will*?
Melissa: *W, L.*
Mary: What letters do you see?
Melissa: *W, A, V, E.*
Mary: Look at the picture. What is the boy doing? What is the car driver doing?
Melissa: They are waving to each other.
Mary: What do you think that word could be?
Melissa: Wave.
Mary: Does *wave* make sense?

Melissa: Yes. "I wave to my friend, the car driver."
Mary: Does "wave to my friend, the car driver" sound right?
Melissa: Yes.
Mary: Does the word look right?
Melissa: The letters make *wave*.
Mary: I like the way you figured that out.

Several things strike me about this exchange. First, the teacher did not directly tell the student anything. Second, the teacher systematically socialized the student's attention to different warrants (evidence and authority) for knowledge and the importance of noticing any conflicts among perceptions and information sources. Third, although the figuring out was collaborative with the teacher playing a primary role, her final comment, "I like the way you figured that out," attributes the accomplishment entirely to the student. This final step offers the student a retrospective narrative about the event in which she stars as the successful protagonist, a collaborative fantasy that makes it possible for the child to become more than herself.

Making Meaning: Making People

When a mother interacts with her baby, she *makes* something meaningful out of what the baby "says." The fact that there is not much to work with does not stop her from constructing a conversation. From "bem ba" she imputes a social intention and responds, "You want milk?" She acts as if the baby's noises are not random but are intentional discursive actions, and responds accordingly. Relationally she positions the baby as a sentient, social being—a conversation partner. In the process, mother and child jointly construct the baby's linguistic and social development and lay the foundation for future interactions with others—how the baby expects to be treated and to interact (Rio and Alvarez 2002; Scollon 2001).

The same is true, in a way, in the classroom. The teacher has to make something of what children say and do. She makes sense for herself, and offers a meaning for her students. She imputes intentions and offers possible worlds, positions, and identities. For example, suppose an independent book discussion group has deteriorated into chaos. The teacher decides to say something to the students. What does she say? Perhaps she says, "That group, get back to work or you'll be staying in

5

at lunch." On the other hand, she might say, "When you are loud like that, it interferes with the other discussion groups and I feel frustrated." On the other hand (yes, teachers have more than two hands), she might say, "This is not like you. What is the problem you have encountered? Okay, how can you solve it?" Each of these responses says something different about "what we are doing here," "who we are," "how we relate to one another in this kind of activity," and how to relate to the object of study. Each different response has the potential to alter the subsequent interactions in the class. The implications of these options are unpacked a bit in Table 1.1.

In other words, language has "content," but it also bears information about the speaker and how he or she views the listener and their assumed relationship. Halliday (1994) calls these the *ideational* and the *interpersonal* dimensions. There is always an implicit invitation to participate in a particular kind of activity or conversation. We cannot persistently ask questions of children without becoming one-who-asks-questions and placing children in the position of the one-who-answers-questions.

Table 1.1: Implications of Different Teacher Responses to Social Transgression

Teacher Comment *Question Answered by Comment*	That group, get back to work or you'll be staying in at lunch.	When you are loud like that, it interferes with the other discussion groups and I feel frustrated.	This is not like you. What is the problem you have encountered? Okay, how can you solve it?
What are we doing here?	Laboring.	Living in cooperation.	Living collaboratively.
Who are we?	Slaves and owner.	People who care about others' feelings.	Social problem-solvers. Normally admirable people.
How do we relate to one another?	Authoritarian control.	Respectful with equal rights.	Work out our problems.
How do we relate to what we are studying?	Do it only under duress.	[no implication]	[no implication]

6

Explicitness

Although language has its effects in many ways, the most common focus of attention in recent years has been on the explicitness of the language teachers use (Delpit 1988; Kameenui 1995; Pressley et al. 2001; Pressley and Woloshyn 1995). Of course, if students need to know something, they shouldn't be reduced to guessing by their teacher's assumptions about what they "should" already know. We often assume that students know things, or know them in particular ways, when they do not. We ask kindergartners, "What is the sound of the letter at the end of the word?," forgetting that many of them are unclear about the concepts *letter, word, sound* (as it applies to speech), and *end* (which requires knowing that letters are ordered left to right), and do not know that letters bear a complex relationship to speech sounds (Clay 1991). As Margaret Donaldson notes in *Children's Minds* (1978), "the better you know something, the more risk there is of behaving egocentrically in relation to your knowledge. Thus, the greater the gap between teacher and learner, the harder teaching becomes."

People who come from different cultural backgrounds often encounter difficulties in their interactions. I recently attended an Indian wedding. Among other blunders, as I proceeded down the reception line, I tried to shake hands with the women in the wedding party, which made them uncomfortable because it is not their normal greeting and because they were not used to such contact with men. Experiences of being in a cultural minority are good for reminding us that different people can do things in very different ways. It is especially easy for mainstream teachers not to notice how difficult it can be for students from a different culture to figure out how things are done here. Those of us in the mainstream are so used to not having to face such conflicts that we come to assume that everyone says and does things the way we do. Consequently, we don't explicitly detail how we do things because one of the rules of conversation is that you don't tell people what they already know (Grice 1975). Minority students often pay a high price for this assumption.

In other words, it is true that we are often less explicit than we might be, that we are confusing sometimes when we try to be explicit, and that being more thoughtfully explicit can be important. Nonetheless, there are many complications to explicitness. We cannot be explicit about everything. The rules of conversation require limiting our explicit comments to what our partner doesn't already know and to what he might find interesting (Grice 1975). This means that deciding what to be explicit about requires some knowledge of our audience—and responsive teachers do have that knowledge of their students (Allington and Johnston 2002b; Johnston et al. 1995).

The assumption that just being more explicit will make for better instruction assumes that language is simply a delivery system for information, a literal packaging of knowledge. It is not. Each utterance in a social interaction does much more work. For example, there are hidden costs in telling people things. If a student can figure something out for him- or herself, explicitly providing the information preempts the student's opportunity to build a sense of agency and independence, which, in turn, affects the relationship between teacher and student. Think about it. When you figure something out for yourself, there is a certain thrill in the figuring. After a few successful experiences, you might start to think that figuring things out is something that you can actually do. Maybe you are even a figuring-out kind of person, encouraging an agentive dimension to identity. When you are told what to do, particularly without asking, it feels different. Being told explicitly what to do and how to do it—over and over again—provides the foundation for a different set of feelings and a different story about what you can and can't do, and who you are. The interpretation might be that you are the kind of person who cannot figure things out for yourself. This is doubtless one reason why recent research has shown that most accomplished teachers do not spend a lot of time in telling mode (Taylor et al. 2002).

As teachers we have to decide *what* to be explicit about for *which* students, and *when* to be explicit about it. Oftentimes, as anyone with teenagers knows, being explicit is the perfect way to meet resistance. The back door is frequently more effective than the front. And of course explicitness doesn't account for some very powerful learning. Very little of our sense of masculinity and femininity, for example, comes about through explicit instruction in the appropriate behaviors, feelings, and values. Our involvements in gendered social-linguistic interactions have much more of an effect (Kondo 1990; Lloyd 1998). I will try (explicitly?) to untangle some of these details in our conversations through this book.

Speech Is Action

Speaking is as much an action as hitting someone with a stick, or hugging them (Austin 1962). A minister, priest, rabbi, imam, or judge, by pronouncing two people husband and wife, make it so (to a point). A teacher naming a child "class poet," inviting her to try on that mantle, can also make it so. The child might then begin assiduously doing the things she thinks poets do. I recall a teacher in an urban high school working with a diverse group of students, responding to the poem one of them had written with, "You really are quite a poet." The student, who until that point had met little success academically, began carrying a paperback book of poetry around in his back pocket and writing more poems. By representing him as a poet, the teacher had opened the door for this student to entertain the possibility of becoming the kind of person who reads poetry and would welcome further interactions based on the premise that he is a poet.

Language, then, is not merely *representational* (though it is that); it is also *constitutive*. It actually creates realities and invites identities. Saying, "You are so smart" is very different from saying, "You are so thoughtful." The phrases invite different views of who I am, and how a person like me behaves. In a classroom, the phrases invite others to view and interact with me differently. Language works to *position* people in relation to one another (Davies and Harre 1999; Langenhove and Harre 1999). For example, a teacher might position himself as the giver of knowledge in the classroom, with the students as receivers of knowledge. A classic (and ubiquitous) example of this is the sequence in which a teacher asks a question to which he already knows the answer, a child answers it, and the teacher announces whether or not the child is correct. Teachers can position children as competitors or collaborators, and themselves as referees, resources, or judges, or in many other arrangements. A teacher's choice of words, phrases, metaphors, and interaction sequences invokes and assumes these and other ways of being a self and of being together in the classroom.

Similarly, the way a teacher talks can position students differently in relation to what they are doing, learning, or studying. The implications of talking about reading as "work" are different from referring to it as "fun." Similarly, telling children they can have free choice time, "but first we have to finish our reading," positions reading poorly simply by using the words "have to." Although language operates within relationships, language practices also influence relationships among people and, consequently, the ways they think about themselves and each other. Language even structures our perception—the sense we make of the neural impulses that come to our brain from our sense organs (Luria 1973;

Neisser 1976). There is no question that "discourse penetrates a fair way into the perceptual system" (Harre and Gillet 1994, p. 169). Just as we actively seek sensory information to inform our construction of reality, we actively seek new information to inform the narrative we are building about who we are and to ensure its genuineness.

In other words, the language that teachers (and their students) use in classrooms is a big deal. My intention with this book is to examine some of the ways in which it is a big deal by exploring words and phrases that turn up in conversations between teachers and their students. These words and phrases exert considerable power over classroom conversations, and thus over students' literate and intellectual development. In the rest of the book, I list various productive phrases and words used (or systematically not used) by teachers and explain why they are significant. I have clustered the words and phrases in what I hope are conceptually useful categories, even though some of them clearly belong in multiple categories. Although these words and phrases are mere fragments of interactions, I think of them as representative examples of linguistic families, in the sense that, though they have different surface forms, they share some common features and common sociolinguistic genetic material (Reichenbach 1998).

My explanations of the significance of these language examples draw on a range of related disciplines, principally discursive psychology (Harre 1998; Harre and Gillet 1994), narrative psychology (Bruner 1994a; Eder 1994; Fivush 1994; Miller 1994), discourse analysis (Davies and Harre 1999; Wood and Kroger 2000), and conversational analysis (Hutchby and Wooffitt 1997). Consistent with these disciplines I assume that each conversational exchange between teacher and student(s) provides building material for children's understanding of a wide range of literate concepts, practices, and possibilities, and helps shape their identities, as each exchange "becomes a fragment of autobiography" (Davies and Harre 1999, p. 38). Readers who are familiar with these disciplines, however, will realize that, from the get-go, I take many liberties. For example, I treat these language fragments as if we can make sense of them outside the immediate context of their use. Of course, we can't. I will try to redeem myself along the way, particularly at the end of the book. In the meantime, I ask that you humor me. (If you are not inclined to humor me, please go to Appendix A for a little more explanation.)

CHAPTER TWO

Noticing and Naming

*Language is the essential condition of knowing, the process
by which experience becomes knowledge.*

HALLIDAY 1993, P. 94

When people are being apprenticed into an activity of any sort, they have to figure out the key features of the activity and their significance. Babies go through a "Wazzis?" (What's this?) stage when they discover that things have consistent names. (Of course they are also learning how to take control of social interactions by asking questions—and learning the fun of doing so.) Noticing and naming is a central part of being a communicating human being, but it is also crucial to becoming capable in particular activities. Becoming a physician requires learning what signs to notice, what to name particular clusters of signs, how to distinguish one drug from another, and how different drugs relate to different patterns of signs. Becoming a teacher requires knowing how to tell when learning is going well and when it is not, what children's invented spelling indicates about what they know, what it means when a child does not participate productively, and so forth. As teachers we socialize children's attention to the significant features of literacy and of learning in different domains.

This pattern recognition is very powerful. Once we start noticing certain things, it is difficult not to notice them again; the knowledge actually influences our perceptual systems (Harre and Gillet 1994). It turns out, too, that there are different ways of naming the same thing. Different schools of healing notice different things and give symptoms different significance. Different schools of teaching do the same. Two teachers with different frameworks of teaching have different names for when a child does not spell conventionally. In some societies there are many words for mental events, in others few. In some communities it is common to talk about and identify feelings. Feelings, too, are socialized—we learn what they are, or rather, we acquire meanings for them. Our bodies respond to events, and in our interactions with others we learn what to make of those emotional responses—what to call them and what sense to make of them, and even whether or not they are something we should talk about. We also learn their relevance. With our assistance, children are expanding and learning to control their own attention, and the attention system is in many ways a "gatekeeper of knowledge acquisition" (Gauvain 2001, p. 70). For this reason I particularly want them to notice language and its significance.

Although noticing and naming things is a central part of apprenticeship, we also learn things without naming them or even really being aware of them. Language is the perfect example. We acquire language, and by the time we arrive at school, we have remarkable facility with it. At the same time, we are largely unaware of it. It is not that children have no awareness. They have been able to lie and tell jokes, for example, for some time, which means they know they can use language to consciously make something different from reality. However, many children graduate high school with little change in their level of awareness, leaving them unprepared to manage the effects language has on them and on others. This leaves them at the mercy of advertisers, politicians, authors, and so forth. It also leaves them unaware of the effects their discursive histories have had on them. Failure to understand these relationships means that they cannot take up issues of social justice perpetuated through language. It is our responsibility to help children notice these things. We can't notice everything, though, and teachers help mediate what is worth noticing and why. This responsibility is worth sharing. Who better to assist than the children themselves? The more they notice and bring to the class's attention the better, and the less the teacher needs to wear the mantle of the one-who-says-what's-important.

From here on in the book, I unpack examples of teachers' talk, showing their effects on individual students and classroom communities. The examples of teacher talk appear as subheadings followed by an analysis of their significance.

✿ *"Did anyone notice . . . ?"*

Part of inviting children to notice is helping them see what kind of things might be noticed, and to name the things being noticed. For example, Did anyone *notice* . . . any interesting words? . . . any new punctuation? . . . any words that are a bit alike? . . . any new ways of arranging words on the page? They can also benefit by attending to their own behavior as they are invited to in, Did anyone *try* . . . some new words they liked? . . . some new punctuation? . . . a different kind of writing? . . . a different kind of reading? Did anyone . . . create a new character? The idea in such questions is to normalize the practice of trying out new possibilities—stretching beyond what one already controls. To notice—to become aware of—the possible things to observe about the literate world, about oneself, and about others can open conversations among students who are noticing different things.

✿ *"I see you know how to spell the beginning of that word."*

When a child has spelled *farm* as *fo*, what is to be said? The most important piece is to confirm what has been successful (so it will be repeated) and simultaneously assert the learner's competence so she will have the confidence to consider new learning. Marie Clay (1993) refers to this as attending to the "partially correct." Its significance cannot be overstated.

Focusing on the positive is hardly a new idea. It is just hard to remember to do it sometimes, particularly when the child's response is nowhere near what you expected. Indeed, the more we rely on expectations and standards, the harder it is to focus on what is going well. I recall being asked once what third graders' spelling *should* be like and wondering how knowing that might help or (more likely) hinder someone's teaching. Certainly, teaching to normative expectations will mean lots of positive feedback for some students (but not necessarily any new learning) and lots of negative feedback for others. Much more important is noticing—and helping the students notice—what they are doing well, particularly the leading edge of what is going well. This leading edge is where the student has reached beyond herself, stretching what she knows just beyond its limit, producing something that is partly correct. This is the launching pad for new learning.

Noticing *first* the part that is correct, or makes sense, is a perceptual bias we need to extend to students. For example, if we ask a student to find a word in his writing that is not quite right and then to mark the piece in it that is right, we can ask him to explore other ways of spelling the part that is not quite right, isolating the problem. We can apply the same principle to a wide range of social and literate practices, such as analyzing group learning processes (as we shall see). I cannot overemphasize the importance of this discursive practice. Children with a solid sense of well-being are less likely to tell stories containing references to negative consequences or negative feeling (Eder 1994). Socializing children's attention to where they are being successful is also likely to develop their sense of self-efficacy (Bandura 1996) or what is increasingly called "agency" (see Chapter 4).

✿ *"Remember the first week when we had to really work at walking quietly? Now you guys do it automatically" (Day 2002, p. 105).*

Often teachers draw children's attention to their learning histories. Showing children that they have changed as community members, learners, readers, and writers reveals that they are in the process of becoming. This category of questions includes ones such as, "How have you changed as a writer?" and "What do you think you need to work on next?" The advantage of drawing attention to change in learning and behavior is that children can then project learning futures. As we shall see in the next chapter, once children have a sense that they are constantly learning, and are presented with evidence of that learning, teachers can ask not only about the detail of their learning histories, but about the detail of their learning futures, and the plans they have for managing those learning futures.

✿ *"What kind of text is this?"*

Asking students to classify a text implies that there are other kinds of text to notice. It opens a conversation about classifying things, including articulating the logic of the classification. For example, you might ask how particular texts are alike or different: "Have you read any other texts like this?" "What is a different text that is on this same theme?" Indeed, Kim Duhamel asked her students to think about what kind of book they were reading, and to "sort yourselves by genre" (Ivey 2002, p. 67), a request that led to discussions of different genre and negotiation of genre boundaries, and an expansion of everyone's understanding of the structure of texts.

In a similar way, Tracy Bennett asked her students, who were studying mysteries in order to write their own, "How are the Bailey School books different from the Boxcar books?" In the ensuing discussion, which included references to TV mysteries, the children explored the different structures of the books and elaborated a chart they had on the organization of mystery stories. In the discussion, Tracy said, "Okay. Talk to us in terms of the elements. So in the beginning, the author introduces the character and then the setting is presented, then certain events take place where clues are provided. That's what I mean by talking in those terms" (Johnston, Bennett, and Cronin 2002a, p. 154). Again, naming and noticing go hand in hand, the naming making it possible to have focused discussions with less confusion.

❦ *"You know what I heard you doing just now, Claude? Putting yourself in her place. You may not have realized it. You said, 'Will she ever shut up?' Which is what Zinny is thinking." (Johnston, Layden, and Powers 1999, p. 20).*
This comment draws to the consciousness of the student and attention of the class, a productive cognitive strategy that would otherwise have slipped by unnoticed. Children, and adults, often accomplish things without any awareness of what they have done. Automatic, fluent performance like this is a very efficient use of mental resources because it doesn't use up our limited conscious space. The downside is that when we encounter problems to which we do not respond so automatically, we can't recall what we did and consider it as a strategic option for the new situation. This comment to Claude describes the mental event and opens the possibility of discussing its significance. It makes the hidden mental skill of the individual into a future resource for both the individual and the community.

This comment actually does a couple of other useful things. It points out (implicitly) to Claude that what he did was a sensible thing to do, as a reader, and offers him the chance to claim competence and agency. It also opens the possibility of discussing the story from Zinny's point of view, and noticing that stories are always presented from a point of view and that some points of view are not given as much prominence as others. In other words, it opens a central conversation for critical literacy.

❂ *"I want you to tell me how it [group discussion] went. . . . What went well? . . . What kinds of questions [were raised]?"* *(Johnston, Bennett, and Cronin 2002a, p. 150).*

This little sequence has several important aspects of noticing and naming. First, Tracy was drawing students' attention to the process of group discussion, which, as we shall see, is critical for both managing and arranging for productive learning zones. Second, asking what went well draws attention first to the productive (agentive) aspects of the process in order to reinforce a solid foundation and build a productive community learning identity. Reviewing the experience as a positive narrative about the group process builds an affinity for this sort of experience. Third, she draws attention to the idea that there are different kinds of questions, just as there are different kinds of text, different kinds of writers, different kinds of words, and so forth, and that noticing them and talking about them is an important part of being literate.

❂ *"Write down a line you wish you had written."*

This request turns children's attention to the qualities of words while it implies (insists, actually) that they all, obviously, want to write wonderful words—to be authors. It opens the possibility that they might be able to write such words, particularly if teachers notice choice words in children's writing or speech. For example, "I notice that your lead is like Patricia MacLachlan's lead in *Through Grandpa's Eyes*" names the concept of lead and shows that it is something that other, perhaps more renowned, authors do, just like the student. At the same time, it gives a name to something, a lead, which can become a topic for subsequent focused discussion.

On another occasion, after rereading a sentence in a read-aloud the same teacher said, "Oh, I love that line" (Johnston and Backer 2002, p. 44). With this comment she does what she asks her students to do. She continues socializing her students' attention to language, opening it up for analysis, but she also expresses a clear emotional response to the language. Studies of teaching often mistakenly neglect teachers' emotional responses. They are important. Even babies use the emotional indicators of their social partner as an important source of information about the environment (Repacholi 1998). Although loving the line is a verbal expression of an emotional response, all interactions are laden with affect, and children attend to these expressions as much as to any other source of information.

❧ *"What are you noticing? . . . Any other patterns or things that surprise you?" (Johnston and Backer 2002, p. 181).*

In Joan Backer's fourth-grade class at the beginning of each day, a student (or some students, or Joan) picked out a word for the day and wrote it on a small white board along with its meaning and diacritical markings—words such as *quagmire*. Early in the afternoon, she covered it up and asked the children to spell the word on index cards. She then put them all up on the chalkboard ledge so they could look at the different ways people had spelled it. She asked them, "What are you noticing?" and then, "Any other patterns or things that surprise you?" (Johnston and Backer 2002, p. 181). She was asking children to examine the logic of words and their spelling strategies, but the assignment to choose an interesting word for the day in the first place had children looking for interesting words, noticing novelty. This alone will expand their range of language. She might have asked them, as another teacher did, to notice also any unusual uses of words. She did ask them in their discussions of poetry, "Are there any favorite words or phrases, or ones you wish you had written?"

Notice how both of these comments assume something about "you"—that you are (obviously, so I don't need to say it explicitly—nor can you contest it) a noticing kind of person. You are (equally obviously) the kind of person who wishes to write interesting things. These are loaded invitations to construct particular identities, which we will return to in the next chapter.

Children becoming literate need to learn the significant features of text, how it is organized (letters, words, arguments, structure, punctuation, and so on), how it relates to spoken language, how to recognize the little tricks authors use to compel readers, when to use which sort of written language, and so forth. However, no learner can afford to be dependent on the teacher for everything that needs to be noticed, so teachers have to teach children to look for possibilities. We draw children's attention to different patterns in texts, words, and sounds, how print is different from illustrations, how it is laid out on the page, and so forth. We will also teach them ways of using these patterns when they notice them, but first they have to notice them. We cannot show them every pattern or feature, and even if we could, we might not want to because we want them to become adept at noticing them for themselves.

When children in class can't help themselves from noticing and pointing out patterns, teaching becomes a whole lot easier. The teacher no longer is the source of knowledge. For example, a second grader in Ellen Adams's class observed, "Did you ever notice that lots of books have wolves in them?" (Adams 1995, p. 115). A first grader in Chris Murphy's class noticed her use of "chitty-chatty" as she drew their attention to the noise level. He pointed out the phonetic similarity of the words and noticed the smaller units of chit-chat. These examples indicate that, in classes like these, children learn that what they notice matters, and that it is a valued topic of conversation. This means that when they notice something, it is worth bringing up for discussion (even at odd times).

Starting with the child's observations rather than the teacher's has many advantages. In studies of infants it is called "attentional following," and infants whose mothers do it develop stronger vocabularies than infants whose mothers constantly try to get their child to attend to something they deem important—requiring "attentional switching" on the part of the infant (Dunham, Dunham, and Curwin 1993; Tomasello and Farrar 1986). When children notice things, instruction can begin with a joint focus of attention because the children are already attending. I once watched Joan Backer do an excellent lesson on handwriting without actually doing a lesson. She explained to her fourth graders that she was having a problem reading some of their handwriting. With a chart of the alphabet in cursive, she invited them to help her plan some instruction to improve their writing, asking them what to start with. She took notes on chart paper as the students brainstormed the problem. In the process, they discussed which were the difficult letters (and what made them difficult), which letters were easily confused (and what made for the confusion), and, for instructional efficiency, which were the most frequent letters (disagreement required a committee to investigate further), and which groups of letters had a lot in common and therefore would get the most instructional mileage. In the process, the children were socializing each other's attention to features of handwriting, and Joan merely cleaned up the details. Classifying the letters also required naming them in terms of their salient characteristics.

The "noticing" question above has a second part to it that is important for other reasons: "Any other patterns or things that surprise you?" The frequent use of "any other" keeps students looking for multiple possibilities, building flexibility, which we will return to later. But the "surprise" part is particularly important. We especially want children to attend to their feeling of surprise, which is a good indicator of conflicting patterns or theories. Such conflicts offer great locations for conceptual learning because they require us to rethink things that we take for granted (Schaffer 1996). Feelings of discomfort or uneasiness can be useful indicators, too. Often, we smother these feelings rather than deal with their source such as when we witness a social wrong.

Marie Clay points out that attending to these feelings is also about building internal control and a self-extending system—a learning system that is self-motivating and self-checking. When children run into trouble while reading and the teacher says, "What's wrong? Something didn't make sense, did it? What can you do?," the teacher is helping them notice those internal signals and contemplate how to respond to them, a system that will continue to operate when the teacher is not there. Helping children use their intuition to learn more about themselves and the world might also help with another phenomenon. According to Winston Churchill, "Men occasionally stumble over the truth, but most of them pick themselves up and hurry off as if nothing had happened" (Brashares 2003). Attending to these bodily feelings of surprise and unease might help us reduce this problem.

Noticing and naming has important implications for critical literacy. Ultimately, children must notice how naming is done, who is named in which ways, and who gets to do the naming. I recall a conversation at our dinner table about the word "skank" in which we discussed what it means, who uses it, why, and what the male equivalent might be. We might call this noticing our naming. We also have to help children, and ourselves, understand how names (as categories) come to be associated with particular definitions. For example, I asked one child, "Are there different kinds of readers in this class?" He responded, "There's ones like the people who's not good and the people who are good" (Johnston 1999, p. 30). His response should give us pause when we say something like, "I am so proud of how you are making sense of what you read and checking to see if the words look right. That is just what good readers do" (Lyons 1991, p. 214). Although the comment points to the strategies the student is using—importantly what the student is doing well, affirming that this kind of problem-solving identifies someone as a *good* reader—it validates the use of a good-bad binary as a sensible descriptor for readers. It leaves open the question of who the bad readers are and how you can tell. A good-bad continuum is not the only way to name readers and writers. In fact, I asked one fourth grader to identify the good writers in class so that I could then ask her about her criteria for distinguishing good writers. Her response was simply, "I don't like to think of it that way." This is tantamount to saying, "That's not a good question and I won't be part of the discussion that it leads to. It's not normal to talk about writers that way." It is the moral equivalent of telling someone of higher social status that they just told a racist joke. Chloe, along with children from similar classrooms, thought that readers and writers come in categories of interest, style, and genre. I know this will be a bit controversial, but perhaps it is better if we say simply, "That is just what readers do."

Through our noticing and naming language, children learn the significant features of the world, themselves, and others. These understandings influence how they treat each other and their environment. For the sake of a just society, I am particularly concerned about children's naming of themselves and others and their awareness of the sources and consequences of those namings.

Extension

To explore this idea of noticing and naming, I recommend books such as Katie Wood Ray's *Wondrous Words* or Ralph Fletcher's *What a Writer Needs* in which they name the details of the author's craft. For example, apply what is discussed in this chapter to the following section from *Wondrous Words* in which a student, Ian, is stuck. In the process of helping him imagine a place to go as a writer, Katie Wood Ray offers to help. They look at his notebook and have the following exchange:

> Katie: Ian, this statement you wrote here, this statement says to me that you have a vignette or a snapshot thing in mind. It sounds like there must be a lot of little scenes in your head about those special times with Jazz [his dog]. Am I right?
> Ian: Yes.
> Katie: I think you could probably play with that structure some and see what happens. You know, a piece about you and Jazz, sort of like Cynthia Rylant's that we looked at, *When I Was Young and In the Mountains* [1982]. Remember how we talked about how it was written with all those little snapshot stories? (p. 259)

She imagines some vignettes as possibilities that jog Ian's memories. Then

Katie: OK, great! You'll need some way of tying them all together eventually, maybe a repeating line like Rylant uses. (p. 260)

She then opens some ideas that get Ian's interest as places to start, and leaves him with a plan:

Katie: I'd do two things, then. First, I'd reread *When I Was Young in the Mountains* to see again how Rylant did this kind of text. Then I'd start a list in your notebook of ideas for little scenes you might write of you and Jazz. OK? (p. 260)

Identity

At the same time that the children were using the stories to proclaim their identity as boys and "tough kids," those stories were also, in a sense, claiming them. That is, the boys were adopting dominant cultural storylines about how tough kids talk.

DYSON AND GENISHI 1994, P. 4

iscussing different authors in his class, Steven observes, "For the funny part, Jessie is really funny. He writes a lot about fantasy stuff. . . . Ron's a pretty good writer . . . and he's a little better at drawing than writing. . . . Emily [in her mystery] gave details. She described the characters. It was a really good mystery because it had a point and it had something that the reader had to figure out" (Johnston, Bennett, and Cronin 2002b, p. 195). In the course of his comments, Steven identifies himself and his peers as authors in the same breath and terms as he talks about the authors of the commercial books they read. His teacher has arranged classroom conversations in which he will develop his understanding of what authors do and further consolidate and elaborate his identity as an author. At the same time, because he sees his peers as a diverse group of authors, and treats them as such, he further consolidates their identities as competent and varied authors. Children in our classrooms are *becoming* literate. They are not simply learning the skills of literacy. They are developing personal and social identities—uniquenesses and affiliations that define the people they see themselves becoming.

When authors write novels, they create characters—people who say this sort of thing, do that sort of thing, and relate to people and things in these sorts of ways. As we come to understand the richness and complexity of a character in a novel, we come to expect how he or she will likely behave when facing a new situation (though new situations can bring surprises). This is not just what authors do, it is what people do with themselves (Bruner 1994a, 1994b; Harre and Gillet 1994; Mishler 1999; Randall 1995). They narrate their lives, identifying themselves and the circumstances, acting and explaining events in ways they see as consistent with the person they take themselves to be.

Building an identity means coming to see in ourselves the characteristics of particular categories (and roles) of people and developing a sense of what it feels like to be that sort of person and belong in certain social spaces. As children are involved in classroom interactions, they build and try on different identities—different protagonist positions. We hear something of this when they use the pronoun "I" in the storylines in which they emplot themselves. As we shall see, they decide not only who they are in a given context, but also between agentive characters who are active and assume responsibility, and more passive characters who do not. They have to take up positions with respect to what they are studying, with respect to others in their social environment, and with respect to domains of practice. Teachers' comments can offer them, and nudge them toward, productive identities.

❧ "What a talented young poet you are."

This family of responses addresses children's developing identities and includes invitations such as, "As scientists, how should we handle this?" To answer the question the child, at least temporarily, has to imagine herself in that identity and might choose to maintain the possibility of wearing that mantle. Notice, again, how the assertion that the students are scientists ("as scientists") is provided as given (already agreed upon) rather than new information, making it much less open to contestation. This kind of conversation requires developing an understanding of what poets (or scientists or mathematicians or authors) do, and the students construct these understandings and ways of talking and acting in the classroom.

Just the identity label will not accomplish all that is needed, of course. In one classroom, the teachers referred to themselves as "senior researchers," and children sometimes as, for instance, "researcher

Tom," and began lessons reiterating that "We are researchers, let us do research" (Elbers and Streefland 2000, p. 39). When children argued that the teacher's role was to tell children the answers, the response was that "It is a characteristic of researchers that they attempt to answer the questions themselves" (p. 41). The response encourages the collective identity of a community of practice, that "people like us" do things this way. It also denies the activity frame presented by the children that "we are traditional students and you are a traditional teacher and we are doing school." It replies, in effect, "I'm sorry but you must be in the wrong theater. I don't know those actors or that plot. Here is how this script goes." It asserts, "When I say 'we' from now on in these conversations, this is the sort of people I am referring to."

Identities such as researcher-in-a-research-community are an important accomplishment of schooling, but also a tool for shaping children's participation in the classroom. These identities provide students with a sense of their responsibilities, and reasonable ways to act, particularly toward one another and toward the object of study. Implicit in these identities are notions of community since identity is tied to both uniqueness and affiliation (Gee 1996). In such classrooms, then, teachers are not merely trying to teach subject matter. Rather, they are, as Elbers and Streefland (2000, p. 37) put it, "mathematizing: turning everyday issues into mathematical problems and using mathematics evolving from these activities for solving realistic problems." Learning science, writing, mathematics, and so forth in this manner breaks the division between school and "the real world," a division that limits the power of children's learning.

❖ *"That's not like you."*

Rather than reprimanding her student, the teacher suggests that the problematic behavior just observed is atypical and that the overall pattern suggests a more admirable person. It invites the child to consider who he wishes to be—and whether he wishes to alter an assumed positive identity. The stronger the relationship between teacher and student, the more powerful and productive this prompt is. Here the function of identity as both a tool and a constantly developing achievement is particularly clear. The teacher is rather like the editor for a writer saying, "The way you have developed the character of your protagonist, he couldn't behave that way in this situation. He's acting out of character."

❖ "I wonder if, as a writer, you're ready for this."

This at once asks the child to think about learning in terms of development or maturity, and invites a desire to be viewed as having an expanded maturity. It leans quite heavily on the student to both view herself as an author, and to pick up the gauntlet of challenge. Interestingly, if she does pick up the gauntlet and overcome the challenge, in the context of the teacher's words it will be hard for her to avoid composing a narrative about self-as-author-overcoming-challenge. Overcoming obstacles in this way provides a seductive invitation to adopt the identity. If the teacher asks her how she did it, she will rearticulate the story—with herself as the successful protagonist.

❖ "I bet you're proud of yourself."

This is most productive after a "how" question that has established agency. Inviting a child to attend to internal feelings of pride builds upon the sense of agency and at the same time attaches an internal motivation to the activity. While building independence it does not detract from the feeling that the teacher is also proud of the child. The more common "I'm proud of you," like other forms of praise, turns a child's attention to pleasing the teacher, rather than developing agency. As with any praise, it positions the child in a subordinate position with respect to the teacher, the source of praise. It also subtly removes some of the responsibility for the accomplishment and gives it to the teacher.

More generally, "How does that make you feel?" turns attention to internal feelings and their relation to behavior and events. For example, asking, "How does it feel to have written a piece like this?" (or "to receive that letter?") has two effects. First is the matter of attaching an internal motivation to the act of writing. The more children notice and rehearse this connection, the better. Rehearsing the connection is almost as good as when it happens and continues to strengthen the connection. The second aspect is that it is part of a central classroom conversation about how x makes y feel. It is part of the responsible side of agency.

❖ "What are you doing as a writer today?"

This query has several features. First, it frames what the student will be doing in terms of what writers do, and invites a conversation on those terms rather than in terms of, say, a student doing a task for the teacher. Second, presenting as "given" the assertions that a) the student is a writer, who b) will be doing something that writers do makes it hard for the student to reject either the identity or the action. They are not up for discussion. The student has to say something like, "[As a writer] I am trying to find a 'hook' for the story I'm writing." The conversation opener insists on a commitment to a particular character (I, a writer) engaged in a particular kind of narrative (doing writerly things). The student is gently nudged—well, all right, pushed—to rehearse a narrative with herself as the writer/protagonist, opening the possibility of the teacher elaborating the story with details and plot suggestions.

❖ *"What have you learned most recently as a reader?"*
As with the previous conversation starter, the teacher begins with "given" information that is not up for discussion: a) the student is a reader, and b) readers learn things. The only question is, what has this particular reader learned? For a student to respond to this question, he or she has to review recent learnings. The opening question requires an answer that begins, "I learned. . . ." It insists on an agentive identity statement about reading and learning. At the same time, it creates a learning history, which is an antidote for students who think they are not good and have always been not good. "What would you like to learn next as a writer?" is a similar question, but it takes the learning history to the next level of agency, creating a trajectory: I learned things in the past and I will learn things in the future, and I have control over those things that I learn. Asking, "How are you going to go about learning them?" extends the agentive conversation even further by insisting that the control of learning belongs to the student, and by turning attention to the strategies that make learning possible.

The overall conversation insists that being a writer entails taking control of learning how to be a better writer. In other words, many of these identity-leaning conversational prompts essentially insist that children respond in ways that position them as active agents in their learning, a topic explored more fully in the next chapter.

Extension

There are two ways to explore your own teaching in terms of children's developing literate identities. The first is to tape-record some class conversations around books and around writing, such as writing conferences, and to listen to them in terms of the issues I have raised in this

26

chapter. A second, perhaps more direct, way is to have conversations with a couple of students in your class around questions such as these:

- Are there different kinds of readers (writers) in this class do you think?
- How do you see yourself as a reader (writer)? (Or) What kind of reader (writer) are you?

To get you started on this project, and in case you do not have your own classroom, I offer the following abstract of a conversation with Mandy. As you read it, ask yourself these questions:

- What noticing and naming are taking place?
- What identity is this student developing?
- What classroom conversations made this identity possible?

As you make your decisions, point to the evidence you are drawing on. Then plan some ways of engaging this student that would alter her understanding of literacy and of herself as a literate person.

Mandy

Mandy says that a good writer "writes fast . . . [For example] when the teacher tells us to write a story then it doesn't even take her . . . not even ten minutes." Mandy does not talk with other students about their writing. She "wouldn't want to hurt their feelings or nothing because sometimes when someone comes up to them and says, 'Oh, you're a bad writer,' and everything. Then, they'll tell the teacher." Mandy says that they should not give other students ideas, "because then that would be giving them things that you thought of in your head. . . . Then they'll have, probably, the same stories."

Good readers, she says, are "all the kids that are quiet and they just listen . . . they challenge themselves . . . they get chapter books." Asked to describe herself as a reader or a writer, she says she doesn't understand the question. She does not know how she could learn about another child as a reader or writer.

Asked whether they do research in her class, she says she is unsure what it is. When it is explained, she says they don't do it. Mandy expects on her report card an "excellent" for writing and a comment like,

"Mandy has behaved and she is nice to other classmates." To help a classmate become a better reader, she would tell him or her to "stop fooling around because the more you fool around, the more you get your name on the board and checks . . . [and] if he doesn't know that word, if he doesn't know how to sound it out or if he doesn't know what it means, look it up in the dictionary."

In talking about books, Mandy makes no connections across books or with personal experience.

CHAPTER FOUR

Agency and Becoming Strategic

A child must have some version of, "Yes, I imagine I can do this." And a teacher must also view the present child as competent and on that basis imagine new possibilities.

DYSON 1999, PP. 396–397

I f nothing else, children should leave school with a sense that if they act, and act strategically, they can accomplish their goals. I call this feeling a sense of agency. Some teachers are very good at building a sense of agency in children, and in this chapter I describe how they do it.

The spark of agency is simply the perception that the environment is responsive to our actions, and many researchers argue that agency is a fundamental human desire (Bandura 1996; Bruner 1994b; Harre and Gillet 1994; Skinner, Zimmer-Gembeck, and Connell 1998). They base this on the fact that even young babies notice and express excitement when their behavior appears to have an effect. They get excited if the mobile above their crib moves when they wriggle. Mothers foster this development when they are responsive to their baby's actions. If mothers are unresponsive to their babies, however, as often happens with depressed mothers, babies lose interest. This desire for agency persists throughout life and is so powerful, that when people feel there is no relationship between what they do and what happens, they become depressed and helpless (Seligman 1975; Skinner, Zimmer-Gembeck, and Connell 1998).

Having a sense of agency, then, is fundamental. Our well-being depends on it. But building this sense does not depend simply on a coincidence between our actions and an event, as it does for babies. For much of what we do there is a delay between our action—such as writing a good lead—and its consequences—drawing people into our writing. Not only is there a delay, but often the consequence is not immediately obvious. People like what we have written, but we have to figure out why; it could have been just a lucky break. This is where the mediation of teachers' language becomes crucial, and where human beings' propensity for storytelling fits in. Teachers' conversations with children help the children build the bridges between action and consequence that develop their sense of agency. They show children how, by acting strategically, they accomplish things, and at the same time, that they are the kind of person who accomplishes things. In Chapter 3, I describe how children might come to think of themselves, for example, as poets. But for the identity to become viable, they have to convince themselves, and others, that they are in fact poets. To do this, they have to convincingly do poetlike things and generate narratives with plots that have them as the poet doing things that poets do, with the anticipated consequences.

The storytelling part gets a boost from the fact that human beings are natural storytellers. We constantly tell stories about ourselves to others and to ourselves, and the stories shape who we think we are. In a sense, we experience ourselves in narrative form, or, as Catherine Riessman (1993, p. 2) puts it, "individuals become the autobiographical narratives by which they tell about their lives." To solve the many problems I will encounter as a writer, and to persist through the many revisions I will face, I have to weave myself into a narrative in which I am the kind of person who encounters and solves problems with text. I develop this belief through a history of conversation with others around my writing.

To understand children's development of a sense of agency, then, we need to look at the kinds of stories we arrange for children to tell themselves. For example, I expect that a child who has a history of telling himself stories about being a failure in writing is unlikely to face a new writing challenge with, "Yes, I imagine I can do this." Similarly, just as we can put ourselves into stories in which we are the active protagonists, the ones with agency, we can plot ourselves in the same story and attribute the agency to another, as in, "The reason my poem was good is that the teacher helped me." Telling such stories in which we relegate ourselves to a passive role is the inverse of agency. Jerome Bruner (1994) calls it "victimicity." Teachers who have worked with students classified as learning disabled will recognize this kind of story as Marie Clay pointed out in her classic paper titled "Learning to be Learning Disabled." There is no question that the way we tell these stories influences academic achievement (Johnston and Winograd 1985; Nicholls 1989; Nolen-Hoeksema, Girus, and Seligman 1986).

The problem for us to solve, then, is how do we arrange for children to tell many literacy stories in which they are the successful protagonists? The heart of a good narrative is a character who encounters a problem and by acting strategically, solves it, usually (but not necessarily) attaining a goal. The following examples of teacher comments are likely to influence the sense of agency children experience in the stories they tell about themselves as literate individuals.

❀ *"How did you figure that out?"*

Asking children this question when they have successfully solved a problem invites them to review the process, or strategies, used to accomplish a goal or solve a problem. The question insists that a child respond with something like, "First I tried to. . . ." In other words, it requires the student to position himself as a storyteller with himself as the protagonist in the story. Aside from the strategy review this provides, it insists that the student adopt an agentive position in the retold narrative. Such a narrative invites a sense of agency as part of the child's literate identity.

This "how did you" invitation to an agentive role is particularly important. We hear a lot about teaching children strategies, but we often encounter classrooms in which children are being taught strategies yet are not being strategic (Ivey, Johnston, and Cronin 1998). Teaching children strategies results in them knowing strategies, but not necessarily in their acting strategically and having a sense of agency. Marie Clay (1991) raises this problem when she talks about teaching *for* strategies rather than just teaching strategies. Teaching for strategies requires setting children up to generate strategies, then reviewing with them, in an agentive retelling, the effectiveness of the strategies they generated, as in, "You figured out that tricky word by yourself. How did you do that?" As children do this, they are in control of the problem-solving process and are asked to consciously recognize that control in an agentive narrative.

This strategy of arranging for a student to figure something out independently, without full awareness, and then reflecting on it, has been called "revealing." Courtney Cazden (1992) contrasts this with "telling," in which the teacher is explicit up front and then the student practices what he has been taught to do by someone else. I suspect that revealing is more difficult than telling because it requires taking into account the child's current understanding. Its benefit is that the child actually does the constructing or problem-solving, which, again, makes possible the development of a sense of agency. Telling, on the other hand, produces metacognitive awareness, which is often quite useful. However, the metacognitive awareness that comes from telling is not always immediately useful. As Clay (2001) points out, "Most things we do as readers need to operate below the conscious level most of the time so that fast and effective processing of the print is achieved and attention is paid to the messages rather than to the work done to get to the message" (p. 127).

The side benefit of the "How did you . . . ?" question is that as children articulate their strategic action, they teach their strategies to other students without the teacher being the authoritative-source-from-which-all-knowledge-comes. It arranges for instruction without hierarchical positioning. Naturalizing this sort of conversation opens the possibility that students will continue such conversations among themselves, thus increasing the level of "explicit" instruction without increasing the extent to which children are being told what to do.

"Sounds good," you might say. "So how do we increase the opportunities to have this sort of conversation?" That's where the next question comes in. To set up agentive narratives, children have to face problems.

✿ "What problems did you come across today?"

When asked as a predictable question this implies that it is normal to encounter problems. Everybody does. This, in turn, makes it normal to talk about confronting and solving those problems. It also helps students identify problems and view them as places to learn, and it sets up the possibility of asking, "How did you solve that problem?" as an invitation to construct an agentive narrative. We can also expand the conversation to "Has anyone else had that problem? How did you solve it?," "How else could we solve it?," and "This is what I do when I have that problem," each of which further expands the agentive possibilities. Of course it is possible for children to answer that they asked someone else how to solve the problem. However, this can be retold asserting the agency of having done so and the need to remember what was learned, before inviting consideration of other options when that one is not available. "Asking someone is a good way to solve a problem; then we know how to solve it ourselves next time. What other strategies could we use?"

Prompts that help children internalize these options will also make them more portable. For example, when a child encounters a problem, asking, "What can you do?" has several benefits. It reminds the student of her agency—"I can do something"—and asks for an exploration of possibilities without actually insisting that they be tried. It is a very different prompt from "Sound it out" or "What would make sense there?" in that it requires the child to be in control of the exploration and selection of strategies, not just the exercise of them. This is part of teaching toward the development of "inner control," freeing the strategy use from the teacher's support (Clay 1991).

✿ *"How are you planning to go about this?"*

Planning means organizing for a productive narrative. It is the most conscious part of being strategic because it happens before we get into the middle of things. It is a very agentive thing to do. Notice that the way this particular question is asked assumes that the student already has a plan. Some students, not having a plan or even having considered the possibility of planning, find the question slightly puzzling, but generate a possible plan and begin thinking about what it would take to enact it. However, planning is not always approached as directly as this. For example, "We need to check our science experiments and our math today. How much time do you think you'll need to finish editing your letters?" This at once models planning—planning is something we do all the time in this class—it gives the children choice over their use of time (although not over what needs to be done), and it requires them to mentally engage in the task analysis that is essential to planning. It really invites them to co-construct a plan for the rest of the afternoon. Planning is imagining a possible agentive narrative that can later be rehearsed through the "How did you . . . ?" and "Did your plan help you?" questions, or in between with, "How are you doing with your plans to . . . ?"

✿ *"Where are you going with this piece [of writing]?"*

This question, like the previous one, is about planning and is forceful because there is no way to answer it simply without accepting the premise. In this case, the premise is that you are in fact going somewhere with the piece of writing (something that might not previously have occurred to you); you have a goal, and possibly a plan. Answering the question requires an agentive narrative. A child faced with the question might not yet have considered the possibility that going somewhere with a piece of writing is something one does. However, the question opens the space for him to imagine such a possibility for this piece, and in the longer term the possibility of acting in that way. It also opens the next step in the agentive conversation, such as, "What are you going to do next to get there?" or "How are you planning to go about this?"

❖ "Which part are you sure about and which part are you not sure about?"

This question, addressed to a student who was aware he had spelled a word incorrectly, redirected his attention to the successful part of his efforts and then focused his problem-solving on the unsolved part, making the problem more focused and thus more tractable. When it was followed by, "How else could you spell that part?," he was able to try options and then recognize the correct version, thus successfully spelling the word. Following this with, "How did you figure that out?" would invite an agentive narrative and a rehearsal of the strategy used.

The first part of the question, though, "Which part are you sure about?" is yet another version of drawing attention to the partially successful and reminds us that the experience of success necessary for developing a sense of agency is partly a matter of perception. Two children might misspell the same word and one will view it as a success and the other as a failure, depending on whether they focus on the erroneous or accurate part of the spelling, or whether they focus on the fact that it had the desired effect on the reader. The language we choose in our interactions with children influences the ways they frame these events, and the ways the events influence their developing sense of agency.

❖ "You really have me interested in this character [in your writing] because of the things he says, and if you show me how he says them and what he looks like, I will get an even stronger sense of him."

This statement, again, draws the child's attention first, and *specifically*, to what has gone well. In particular, though, it shows what went well through its *effect* on the audience, showing the agency of authorship.

This gets around the need for praise, which can build dependencies, and allows the developing writer to understand how to tell for himself whether his efforts were or will be successful.

However, pointing out to a student what worked well is not enough. Teaching requires moving beyond that to what is next for the student's development. Knowing the importance of this second step, we are inclined to say, "You really have me interested in this character [in your writing] because of the things he says, but you haven't. . . ." In this construction, the one word, *but*, effectively undermines the first piece of feedback. It is the *and* in the first part of the quote that is critical. Notice that not only is the affirmation in the first part left intact, but that the remainder of the sentence is likely to be "and if you, . . . then . . ." In other words, this structure sets up a possible future, including an audience consequence, a strategy that leads to it, and a narrative with the student in the position of protagonist or agent. At the same time it opens this door, the conditional *if* does not force the child through it. The one word, *and*, changes the entire structure of the interaction, affecting the motive for actually engaging the feedback and the implications for the child's identity.

This is not to ignore the value of *but*, which has a different function, one of presenting a conflict for resolution. For example, "*went* would make sense (affirmation), but what letters would you expect if it were *went*?" Such prompts are intended to pose a problem for the learner to solve, often requiring some reorganization of cognitive processing (Clay 2001). Notice, though, that the affirmation still comes first. Notice, too, that although the affirmation has some of the qualities of praise, it is quite different. It attributes the source of the productive aspect to a warrant (makes sense) that the child is assumed to have used. Whether or not the child used the warrant, the retelling implies it in a way that makes the attribution difficult to reject. Actually, warrants like this are a critical part of persuasive storytelling, and some children need serious persuasion to desert their old unproductive stories. Perhaps you have come across this in parts of your own life.

I should not leave the quote without also describing the importance of *if* ("and if you . . ."). There is a real difference in a writing conference between saying, "If you were to add information about the cat, where would you put it?" and "Put in more information about the cat" (Graves 1994). One leaves open the choice of actually doing it, but insists on rehearsing the thinking behind it (the important instructional piece) and the other leaves no choice—and a reduction in agency. In fact the question and the imperative have very different implications for motive, agency, and identity.

❧ *"That's like Kevin's story. He started off telling us his character is a lonely boy to get us caring about the main character. You [looking at Kevin] made a conscious choice"* *(Johnston, Bennett, and Cronin 2002a, p. 155).*

The key word in this fragment is "choice." Choice is central to agency. Making a choice requires one to act—preferably to deliberate and act. Often we do things in particular ways, or see things through particular perspectives, forgetting that there are options. This particular comment has even more to recommend it. By connecting his work to that of a published author whose work the students admire, it clearly announces Kevin as an author, showing evidence for the parallels that support the connection, and reminds Kevin, and the class at the same time, that authors make decisions and should consciously contemplate them. It invites the class to treat Kevin as an author and to break down any barriers between other, more published authors and authors like Kevin. While valorizing Kevin as an author, with agency and power, this is not simply praise. It is information provided in a way that makes public recognition possible without some of its side effects. In public settings praise for an individual always runs the risk of "unpraising" others. "Good" can be praise, but when it follows "wonderful" to another student, it can be "faint praise."

The "choice" aspect of the comment also leads to a productive narrative about the nature of the choosing process. For example, "I notice you chose to write about this as a poem. How come?" insists on a narrative about the grounds for an authorial decision, requiring an articulation of something that might have been an unconscious process. At the same time, it requires the student to don an author's identity to give the narration, and opens a broader conversation with the class about choices among genres, and the grounds for making such choices.

Choice is important to foreground in classroom interactions because sometimes children behave in unsatisfactory ways. The first step in rehabilitation for the long term is to remind them that their behavior reflects a choice, and to help them think through the alternatives and their consequences. Imagining making different choices helps a lot. Sometimes children do not see something as a choice because they cannot imagine the options. It's just something that they do. This is when we pose "Suppose . . ." or "What if . . ." possibilities for them, or open new possibilities by connecting them to other sources. For example, we might ask, "How would [familiar author, respected other, etc.] handle this?," "How about [another familiar author, respected other, etc.] . . . ?" These questions turn children's attention not only to the need for conscious choice, but also to possible sources for imagining options. This kind of conversation is directed toward building and connecting what Jerome Bruner (1986) calls the "dual landscapes" of consciousness and action.

❧ "Why . . ."

"Why" questions are the essence of inquiry. Once young children latch onto "why" questions, they come to see how useful they are for getting to the bottom of how (some) things work and finding the limits of others. Aside from being the basis of at least one side of science and of logic, "why" questions also develop children's persuasion and argumentation abilities, and logical thinking. They have the potential to help children balance emotional and rational dimensions of literate life.

"Why" can also be applied to the logic of behavior and decisions as an invitation to review and make conscious a process and its associated values. Asking why children do or say the things they do helps them develop the consciousness and hence ownership of their choices. It brings to consciousness the feelings, intentions, relationships, motives, logic, values, and plans that lie beneath action and are the hidden levers of narrative. "Why" questions have the same effect when applied to the actions of characters in books, particularly when deliberate connections are made to the child's own life, as in questions such as, "Why do you think she would do that?" The same principle can be applied to classroom discussion of critical incidents, which gives the added advantage of increasing the available interpretive frames from which to choose. Perhaps more important, they can also be applied to authors in general, as in the next question.

❧ "Why would an author do something like that?" (Johnston, Bennett, and Cronin 2002a, p. 155).

This question asks students to view writing as fundamentally intentional and rife with decisions. Naturalizing conversations about the intentional nature of writing provides the grounds for critical literacy. It opens the possibility of making word choice, ideology, and private inter-est important when reading. It also requires the child, as a reader, to imagine himself into the writer's role, building a bridge between read-ing and writing that helps to generalize what is learned in one to become useful in the other. Imagining oneself into another writer, how-ever, requires a social imagination, to which I will return presently.

Imagining why an author made a particular choice opens the possi-bility of doing things differently, so that it is possible to ask, "How else could she [the author] have done that?" Of course this can also be asked with respect to the student's own writing, as in, "How could you have done that differently?" Both together build the necessary links between reading and writing. "Why did the author choose that word?," "What other words could he have used?," and "Do you think when he used that word to describe Rob [a character], it changed the way we thought about him?" are all part of a systematic attempt to insist that students take the intentionality and political nature of authorship as a given. Once this has been established, it becomes possible for children to read against the author's intentions. It becomes possible, and more likely, for them to read critically. Within these conversations, children can start to imagine what a writer has systematically left out—voices, perspectives, details—and to exercise control over their reading. Other children's per-spectives routinely voiced in the classroom also have a powerful influ-ence on this, as we shall see presently.

Powerful Narratives

The comments in this chapter are all invitations to construct a retelling of an event from an agentive position. Naturalizing such questions leads to the unspoken assertion that trying, struggling, noticing, and creating are normal, expected things to do. Underlying all of these conversations, of course, are relationships and evidence that support the narrative and make it trustworthy and persuasive. Students have to be convinced that our words are real and not empty flattery, and the evidence is in the details and in their manner of presentation.

Sometimes there is real risk in accepting agency. When a learner has built a narrative around his unsuccessful experiences in literacy that puts him in a passive role, there is no responsibility for failure. Accepting an agentive role can also be risky in the context of blaming conversations. This is a reason for building agency around successful events initially, and why arranging for events to be successful in the first place is fundamental. Nonetheless, the handling of potentially negative episodes is crucial, too, because they often have a pivotal role in narratives. First, negative episodes must be thought of as expected and useful. This is why "What problems did you encounter today?" is so important to naturalize. But when a child tries something and does not succeed, we need to turn that event toward a narrative and identity that will be useful for the future. If children are not making errors, they are not putting themselves in learning situations.

It is common enough for children to produce writing drafts with no spelling errors because they do not want to risk what they think of as failure. We can limit this possibility by overtly valuing children's exploration of new tactics and possibilities. For example, "Did anyone try any new or difficult words in their writing today? . . . Great! Tell us about it. . . . That's what William Steig does when he writes—uses interesting words. Did anyone else try anything new or different?" We can also help students reframe the sort of story a negative episode represents—how it might play a role in their identity as a learner, writer, reader, citizen: "Yes, you did have trouble with that, but I really like the way you are challenging yourself." Drawing children's attention to their successes and showing them how their decisions and strategic actions were responsible for them increases children's perceptions of their ability and the effectiveness of their focused efforts (Pintrich and Blumenfeld 1985). Drawing their attention to their effort ("You worked really hard at that") or their intellect ("You are so smart") will not generate sufficiently useful narratives.

As teachers, then, we try to maximize children's feelings of agency. There are really three parts to this: the belief that the environment can be affected, the belief that one has what it takes to affect it, and the understanding that that is what literacy is about. An organized and predictable classroom helps a great deal with the first of these, as does arranging for children to be successful. However, we can affect both by ensuring that the narratives in which we immerse children emphasize the agentive nature of literacy, and their particular agentive roles. We know that this is effective because the most successful interventions for improving children's feelings of agency in academic domains have included not just teaching effective strategies, but also using attribution retraining in which children are helped to tell agentive stories about their performance. These interventions have improved not only children's sense of agency, but also their engagement in and motivation for subsequent academic activities (Foote 1999; Schunk and Cox 1986; Skinner, Zimmer-Gembeck, and Connell 1998).

It might already have occurred to you that children bring with them to school well-learned cultural narratives acquired in cooperatively retelling family stories from a very young age. These narratives hold models of the possible forms narratives can take, who is allowed to take which roles, and so forth (Pontecorvo and Sterponi 2002). Children have already learned some of the roles open and not open to girls, the feelings and actions that go along with those roles, and how certain behaviors should be understood, such as a boy who reads or a girl who argues. They have learned these aspects of agency in subtle ways. For example, mothers tend to retell events differently to daughters and sons, particularly when it comes to emotional events. An event reconstructed as invoking sadness for a daughter, such as having a toy stolen, is likely to be reconstructed to include anger for a son (Fivush 1994)—emotions with very different relationships to agency. In school, it is our job to help expand the possible agentive narrative lines available for children to pick up.

Boys and girls differ, too, in the stories they tell about success and failure. Boys learn to tell stories in which they claim agency for their academic successes but not their failures, whereas girls tend to tell stories with the opposite attributions. They experience success and failure through these powerful culturally derived narratives (Bruner 1994b). Our job is to change these narratives so that both boys and girls have a productive sense of the implications of the choices they make and the strategies they choose. We do this by foregrounding these in the agentive narratives through which we help them reconstruct the events.

Agency Matters

Developing in children a sense of agency is not an educational frill or some mushy-headed liberal idea. Children who doubt their competence set low goals and choose easy tasks, and they plan poorly. When they face difficulties, they become confused, lose concentration, and start telling themselves stories about their own incompetence. In the long run they disengage, decrease effort, generate fewer ideas, and become passive and discouraged. Children with strong belief in their own agency work harder, focus their attention better, are more interested in their studies, and are less likely to give up when they encounter difficulties than children with a weaker sense of agency (Skinner, Zimmer-Gembeck, and Connell 1998). Feeling competent, these children plan well, choose challenging tasks, and set higher goals. Their concentration actually improves when they face difficulties, and in the process of engaging difficulties they learn more skills. Of course the whole process is cyclical because these relationships are reflected in their academic success, which then reinforces their sense of agency. When children decide that they have no agency with respect to their learning, their learning is limited in terms of both personal experience and potential trajectory. Performance differences between children with a stronger and weaker sense of agency continually diverge, particularly from fifth grade on.

The concept of agency in literacy and learning is not only central for the individual's sense of competence and well-being, and for his or her performance (Eder 1994; Ivey, Johnston, and Cronin 1998; Skinner, Zimmer-Gembeck, and Connell 1998), but also indispensable to democratic living, though individual agency is not enough for that. As we shall see in Chapters 6 and 7, both individual and collective agency are important to develop because there are many situations in which an individual cannot have a major influence and because collective agency offers the possibility of developing an identity through affiliation. Both independence (an aspect of agency) and belonging are documented contributors to children's classroom engagement (Blumenfeld 1992; Roeser, Midgley, and Urdan 1996; Wentzel 1997).

Extension

Analyze the following transcripts in terms of their invitations to agency and see whether there are ways to enhance them.

Transcript 1

Bill: You worked hard on this page. Where was the tricky part?
[*The student points to the word* through.] Look at the picture and tell me what she did.
Peter: She went over the fence.
Bill: It could be *over*, but check to see if what you read looks right.
Peter: No, it's not *over.*

Bill: How do you know?

Peter: There's no *v*.

Bill: Good checking. What would make sense?

Peter: I don't know.

Bill: Would *through* make sense?

Peter: Oh, yeah—"through the fence."

Transcript 2

Kathy: Today's story is called *Cat on the Mat.* Look at the last
   word in the title; that word is the same as your name, isn't it?

Matt: I don't know.

Kathy: Sure it is; your name is Matt, isn't it? And this word is
   mat, except this word only has one *t* instead of two *t*'s like in
   your name. I will read you the story and you read along. "The
   cat sat on the mat. The goat sat on the mat. The cow sat on
   the mat. The elephant sat on the mat. SSppstt." Can you
   sound out those letters?

Matt: *Sssssss. Tttt.*

Kathy: Good. I'll finish the book now: "The cat sat on the mat."

Both these transcripts are from the exceptional book *Partners in
Learning: Teachers and Children in Reading Recovery* (Lyons, Pinnell,
and DeFord 1993) pages 162–163 and 151, respectively. Although there
are some productive examples of teacher talk in the first transcript, both
examples are shown in that book to be problematic. The first is problematic because the teacher did not realize that Peter had lost track of
characters and thought that *she* referred to the fox. The second is problematic because of the text/task difficulty and because of the teacher's
conception of reading instruction—what she was trying to do. She was
trying to get the student to recognize and sound out words that were
beyond her student's capability rather than trying to arrange for him to
take control of reading the book.

Flexibility and Transfer (or Generalizing)

A colleague tells a story about his daughter learning to write. Her teacher tells him in a conference that she is doing badly at writing in school. My colleague protests that she writes wonderfully at home; however, the teacher shows him examples of her school writing that, he concedes, confirm the teacher's view. He takes the matter up with his daughter, who is genuinely surprised that the two activities are related in any way. What she knows about writing at home does not seem at all relevant to school writing. I have certainly had this experience with children, especially in math. Strategies used to calculate area for a math quiz seem to have no relevance when the child is faced with calculating garden space. Children often know things from their writing that they fail to use when solving problems in reading. Some children keep home and school spaces rigidly separate, believing they are unrelated. The stories they tell in these different life spaces are different—different genres, settings, characters, and goals.

These are problems of transfer—the failure to generalize learning from one situation or problem to another. Teachers and other researchers of all stripes have puzzled over this problem for a long time. However, in some classrooms children quite flexibly generalize what they have learned. For example, in one classroom children had been using the strategy of "stepping into" characters—taking their perspective. One of the children then did this in science as they studied ducklings. He hypothesized about the basis for the duckling's behavior by taking the duckling's perspective. When he did this, another child, used to looking for such parallels, noticed and pointed out to the class what he had done. It seems that the less compartmentalized we make children's learning lives, the more likely they are to transfer their strategic problem-solving to other situations. These children were also flexible in the ways they applied strategies to solve a given problem. Rather than repeating the same strategy, or quitting, they were likely to use multiple strategies. What makes this possible? How do teachers build bridges between activity settings, making it so that the agency a child exercises in writing transfers to her reading or math? How do they get a child to apply strategies flexibly and in new situations?

Actually, a lot of the conversations we have already discussed have implications for flexibility and transfer. For example, encouraging children to entertain certain identities can help. Consider this. A study compared the arithmetic learning of a group of high school students apprenticed to shopkeepers with that of a group of shopkeepers. Both groups were taking an adult education class to improve their arithmetic (Beach 1995, cited in Cobb and Bowers 1999). Which group would you predict to be more successful at learning arithmetic? It turns out that the shopkeepers were more successful at transferring their learning to their out-of-class shopkeeping lives, most likely because they held the same goals and activity frames in and out of class. In both situations they had the same goal: making their business more profitable. The high school students, on the other hand, had different goals in the two settings: acquiring knowledge in one setting, generating a profit in the other. This helps explain why children who learn words for their spelling test commonly don't transfer the learning to their writing. Once a child incorporates into his identity a sense that he is a writer doing writerly things (or a scientist, mathematician, and so forth), he can ask himself in a new situation (not necessary consciously) what he might do *as a writer*, since those roles do not stop at the border of a single activity setting. Imagining oneself as the writer of a piece can also help transfer writing experience to one's activities as a reader.

The following few examples of teacher talk are ones that we have not yet encountered, but that serve to encourage transfer and flexibility.

❖ *"One of the things people do when they start a story is think of what they know. Mathematicians do this too. . . . Let's try it." (Allington and Johnston 2002a, p. 180).*

44

Reminding children to begin a new activity by taking stock of what they already know (in current mechanistic terms "activating prior knowledge") has several functions. First, it reduces the magnitude of the problem to be solved. Second, it puts the new problem in the context of old, already-solved problems. Third, it opens the possibility of more connections among the new knowledge and what is already known. However, this particular invitation takes a couple of extra steps. It represents the kind of problems readers face as similar to those that mathematicians face, encouraging active transfer of a strategy across what would otherwise have seemed to be quite different activities. The ability to solve new problems flexibly depends on how the problem is viewed in the first place—whether the strategic demands are seen as similar to other, familiar problems (Kuhn et al. 1995). The invitation encourages children to increase the boundaries within which they look for problem similarities, stretching beyond the surface structure of activities to more metaphorical levels. The "let's" is also important in this regard. Collaborative problem-solving helps break down the boundaries between different tasks because a collaborator can bring a different perspective to a problem, reframing it so that it is more like a familiar one. More on this later.

❖ *"How else . . ."*

It is wonderful when a child solves a problem. We can then ask her to regale us with the story of how she solved it, building her sense of agency. After having done that is the perfect time to ask how *else* she might have solved it. Doing so sustains the possibility of choice (and thus agency) while maintaining a sense of flexibility—there's always another way. Even with less successful experiences it is possible, after pointing to what went well, to consider options with questions such as, "Is there anything you might do differently?," which emphasizes choice retrospectively—like revising and editing. Such questions are a bit more risky, though. They require a secure relationship within which exploration of past decisions is interesting and not grounds for blame.

Else is a very powerful word. It simultaneously builds flexibility and implies a range of other important messages. For example, "How else could the author have said that?" not only builds a flexible approach but also reminds students that writing is always intentional and, implicitly, that it is always consequential. To bring the implicit reminder forward we might ask how saying it that way would change a reader's interpretation. In a similar way, "What else do you think they [audience] would like to know?" opens possibilities for inclusion in a piece of writing, but at the same time, reminds the young writer of his responsibilities to his audience. It is also a reminder that writers always make choices about what they include and exclude from their writing— what they choose to tell and not tell. Taking this concept back to children's reading opens a central conversation for critical literacy: What is the author not telling us? Whose perspectives are not represented? and so forth.

❧ *"That's like . . ."*

The word *like* has two primary functions. It draws attention to connections (with other experiences, books, authors, situations, practices, words, and so forth) and it makes metaphors, both of which are fundamental not only to transfer, but also to understanding and reasoning. Connections are at the heart of comprehension or understanding. They provide anchors and retrieval routes. The more connections, the more flexibly something can be accessed.

Transfer involves overcoming apparent dissimilarities between activities. For example, reading Web pages and reading a book are sufficiently different to limit the extent to which children might transfer what they have learned to do in one to their activities in the other. The same might be said of different genres of writing or of reading and writing. Increasing transfer primarily involves simply overcoming these apparent dissimilarities and encouraging children to ask what ways one activity, problem, or role, is like another. This means thinking beyond the literal to the metaphorical, and the word *like* is very good for invoking metaphors. We want children to ask themselves not only "What do I know about this?" but "What do I know that is like this?"

At the same time that thinking metaphorically helps with transfer, it has other benefits. Metaphors provide new ways of understanding and deepening meaning, "stand[ing] with one foot in the known, while placing the other in the unknown." They are what Judith Lindfors (1999, p. 170) calls "reaching devices." For example, teaching about parallel circuits, June Williamson (Wharton-McDonald and Williamson 2002, p. 92) explains that "electricity finds another way to go. Kind of like when you're caught in traffic: Sometimes you can find another path around the jam." A series circuit she likens to the World Series: "One game after another. And if you lose a game, you're out."

Indeed, Brian Sutton-Smith (1995, p. 87) refers to the mind as fundamentally *multi-metaphoric*, observing that young children are very competent with metaphoric thought. He points out that "once children can speak, they move endlessly through the vocalized plural play of metaphor." As an example, he reports watching his two-year-old granddaughter playing in a sandpit, "first pouring the sand and calling it Coke, and then rounding it and calling it an egg, and then lengthening the shape and calling it a sausage, and then banging and slapping it with a vocalized rhythm which she called a song, and so on. The properties of the material in the child's hands were 'poured' through a vocal string of metaphoric signifiers." Along with Bateson (1979), Sutton-Smith argues that metaphor is essential to the evolution of thought, which advances by finding similarities among forms.

The word *like* has other incidental properties, too. When applied to people it emphasizes our common humanity over our individual and cultural quirks and is thus productive in terms of building a caring, tolerant community. However, because *like* draws comparisons, it also raises the possibility of noticing contrasts, absences, and disjunctures. These are the crucial foundations not only of problem formation and learning, but of critical literacy. We can ask about similarity and difference in the treatment of others, for example.

❊ "What if . . . ?"

Thinking flexibly and metaphorically involves expanding the imagination, and what-if questions insist on an imaginative act. What-if questions can be used to expand the contexts in which particular strategies might be used, or particular identities might hold sway. Because we can't routinely be presented with multiple contexts, we help children do mind experiments to think themselves into other situations and try out their learning or strategies, making the necessary accommodations. For example, after a child has told us how he managed to research the characters for his historical fiction piece, we might ask, "What if you were writing a science report? Would any of these strategies help there?"

"What-if . . ." and "suppose . . ." invitations have additional benefits. They develop children's ability with hypothetical talk and abstract thinking. They are the foundation of mind experiments and give children the chance to understand the possibility of multiple versions of reality. These abilities are fundamental to both productive individual choice and to negotiating collaboratively productive meanings and solutions as

47

required for democratic living. At the same time, these questions develop children's argumentation skill, particularly because they invite "if . . . then . . ." statements and the thinking that lies behind them. What-if questions used in the context of narrative can also develop children's understanding of narrative structure, because the questions require construction of alternative possibilities using narrative logic.

These hypotheticals can be used to explore worlds, behaviors, and choices without real consequences. Don Graves (1994) points out that posing the hypotheticals such as, "Suppose you were going to put some dialogue into this story. Where would you put it?" can produce the necessary learning without the resistance that might come from the anticipated effort needed to actually do it. It opens the imaginative possibility, and accomplishes the necessary instruction without risk. Of course, once the possibility is imagined, it can be tempting to actually do it.

Hypotheticals are the stuff of invention. They are also a useful way into critical literacy since they can provide a way of stepping out of the known and taken-for-granted. For example, a discussion of the disparity in pay between male and female athletes reveals that many children find it perfectly reasonable. However, when asked, "What if your mother were an athlete?" most of the children suddenly find it unreasonable. Mind experiments like this can allow us to notice things that are otherwise too naturalized to be noticed, and help us use our experience to understand possible events we have not experienced.

❧ *Playful language.*

I should not leave the topic of flexibility and transfer without a comment on playfulness. Language play takes the pressure off language and literate practice and invites experimentation with alternative practices and realities. Writers such as Dr. Seuss clearly understand this. Play and playful use of language of all kinds can be particularly productive. There are few better ways to draw children's attention to the structure of words and texts than through language play and parody. Freed of the burden of meaning, nonsense rhymes and the like reveal the internal structure of words as an object of interest rather than of labor. Parodies do the same at the text level. Indeed, Sutton-Smith (1995) reminds us of Vygotsky's stance on play in which we should

> imagine two girls who are sisters playing a game called "two girls who are sisters," as an exemplification of the way in which rule

structures are first engendered in play, so that meaning arises and abstracts itself from everyday contextualization. He says, "From the point of view of development, creating an imaginary situation can be regarded as a means of developing abstract thought" (Vygotsky 1978, p. 103). If this should be true, and it may well be, it means that play has a direct, not an indirect, relationship to cognition. (p. 72)

Following Bakhtin, Sutton-Smith (1995, p. 71) observes that "laughter is the most primitive form of parody and satire by which the sanctity of established ways gets impugned. It is life's basic form of unofficial response." In other words, it is a good vehicle for flexibly breaking rules and borders. As a vehicle for progressing to critical literacy, playfulness with language might also be indispensable.

An additional benefit, as I mentioned at the outset, is that playfulness can develop children's interest in language. For example, having read William Steig's *The Amazing Bone* (1976) with students it becomes possible for me to add into my classroom vocabulary "As I live and flourish . . ." and to stop inappropriate behavior with "Have you no shame, sir!" or, better, "You worm, you odoriferous wretch!" or even "Yibbam sibibble!" These latter can be used to admonish because children's awareness of the source makes their use funny, taking the personal edge off the reprimand. At the same time, it builds the children's vocabulary and their interest in language, and shows them an excellent resource for further language development.

A Longer Example

At this point, I think we should put some of the brief snippets of language into context, so let me give another elaborated example of a teacher-student interaction that pulls together much of what I have already presented. Consider this transcript of a writing conference taken from an excellent book called *How's It Going?* by Carl Anderson (2000).

> Carl: You know, Maya, you're just like a lot of writers who write memoirs. Like Jean Little, for example. You know that story from *Little by Little*, the one in which her classmates make fun of her because of her eyeglasses?
>
> Maya: Yeah.

Carl: Both you and Jean Little packed several scenes into a single piece of writing. But Jean Little didn't just stretch the first scene and list the rest. She stretched most of the scenes, the scenes that really helped us understand what she went through. You could revise by trying to make your memoir more like the ones you've read in class so far this year. That's what I want you to try—picking one of these other scenes and stretching it like you stretched the birthday candles.

Maya: Okay.

Carl: Which one would you want to try?

Maya: Maybe . . . I kind of like it the way it is.

Carl: I can understand that. But I'm still going to challenge you to take a risk as a writer by trying out Jean Little's way of stretching several scenes. And if you decide you don't like what it does to your piece after trying it, that's okay. . . . I nudge students to try things I think will help them grow as writers. So which scene do you want to stretch—the scavenger hunt, the sleeping routine, your mom tucking you in . . .

Maya: I think my mom tucking me in.

Carl: [*starts her on a new piece of paper*] I'll check in with you later in the period to see how it goes (pp. 77–78).

This conference is really quite forceful, but when Carl returns to Maya, she is satisfied with the outcome and chooses to make use of the new writing she produced. The chart on the following pages reviews in tabular form what I see as significant pieces of this conference.

Perhaps it seems in places as though I am stretching the intentions and the implications. I don't believe so, but if even half of my inferences are true, repeating these discursive currents over and over each day cannot help but have a powerful effect, the more so because it is not only Carl who is applying this discursive pressure toward agentive narratives. Once these conversations become natural in the classroom—ways of talking and interacting that imply roles, relationships, positions, authority, agency, epistemology, topics of conversation, and expected identities—they also become part of children's conversations.

In this chapter and the previous one I have emphasized the kinds of conversation that encourage children to become agentive, to act for themselves and see themselves as active and thus responsible. In part, this involves recognizing multiple ways of seeing and solving problems,

Carl's Talk	Commentary
Maya, you're just like a lot of writers who write memoirs.	Carl offers a specific identity: authors who write memoirs. He names memoirs as a kind of writerly thing to notice.
Like Jean Little . . . that story from *Little by Little,* the one in which her classmates make fun of her because of her eyeglasses?	Carl uses a specific example to show that the identity claim is not empty praise. It shows the parallel between the writing and the writers, but also between the two lives. *Like* also becomes more normalized as a way of talking and thinking.
Both you and Jean Little packed several scenes into a single piece of writing.	Carl extends the evidence for the identity and opens a possibility for Maya's life and text narratives, and establishes the equivalent epistemological authority. He names "scenes" as something to be noticed—analyzing the task.
But Jean Little didn't just stretch the first scene and list the rest. She stretched most of the scenes . . .	Carl articulates and names the process used by the mentor author and notes that it is one Maya has already used—further task analysis.
that really helped us understand what she went through.	Carl shows the consequences of the author's use of the process/strategy, and the agentive, intentional nature of writing.
You could revise by trying to make your memoir more like the ones you've read in class . . .	Carl opens an agentive possibility for Maya's writing along with an identity challenge.
That's what I want you to try—picking one of these other scenes and stretching it like you stretched the birthday candles.	Using positional authority, Carl requires Maya to pick up the challenge, retelling the previous agentive narrative to maintain the sense of agency. The task analysis maintains choice and opens the possibility for later strategic planning in writing.
Which one would you want to try?	Carl offers choice, and thus agency in the process, but constrains the possible narratives.
I can understand that. But I'm still going to challenge you to take a risk as a writer by trying out Jean Little's way of stretching several scenes.	Recognizing Maya's expression of her own agency, Carl adds to his positional authority the challenge to the identity already offered. This is an offer of a narrative with a specific identity and a challenge to overcome. If she picks up this challenge, she cannot help but pick up the authorial identity. To the extent that the identity is inviting, the narrative is inviting.

. . . if you decide you don't like what it does to your piece after trying it, that's okay . . .	Carl offers Maya a narrative in which she can regain the agency he has temporarily taken away by limiting her choices.
I nudge students to try things I think will help them grow as writers.	Reminding Maya of his role as a teacher, Carl reminds Maya of her identity as a writer, but "help them grow" indicates that she also has an agentive role in her growth.
So which scene do you want to stretch— the scavenger hunt, the sleeping routine, your mom tucking you in . . .	"So now that you have agency as a writer and a learner, how do you want to retell your life narrative?" Carl offers specific choice, and hence agency. With the specificity is the recognition that he is interested in Maya's life details, strengthening his relational position and Maya's authority.
I'll check in with you later in the period to see how it goes.	In case Maya decides to abandon the offered narrative, Carl at once closes the door on the lesser narrative and shows interest in her personally and as a writer.

and a certain relish in doing so. If we fail to accomplish this, it does not bode well for them once they leave the educational environment. Unfortunately, it remains possible (perhaps even common) for learners to leave school believing that they know a great deal yet unable think for themselves, not seeing themselves as active, inquiring individuals. The more we help children build a sense of themselves as inquirers and problem-solvers, and the less they see boundaries between domains of inquiry, the more they are likely to transfer their learning into the world beyond school.

Even this is not enough. I want children to see themselves not only as inquiring individuals, but as inquiring individuals who are part of a diverse community that inquires, whose members, through their active participation and diversity of perspective, contribute to each other's intellectual growth. It is to this aspect of teachers' talk that I now turn.

Knowing

At its deepest reaches, education gave me an identity as a knower. It answered the question "Who am I?" [but it also answered the question] "what is the world?" . . . and the same knowledge that gave me a picture of myself and the world also defined the relation of the two. . . . What is the nature of the knower? What is the nature of the known? And what is the nature of the relations between the two? These questions belong to a discipline called epistemology.

PALMER 1993

The common pattern of interaction between teachers and their students has been called the IRE for teacher Initiates, student Responds, and teacher Evaluates (Cazden 2001; Coulthard 1977), or sometimes IRF (for Feedback, see Wells 2001). For example, consider the following interaction (Johnston, Jiron, and Day 2001, p. 226; T = teacher, S = Student):

T: We have been working all year on what is called sequence.
   What does sequence mean? [I]
S: Order? [R]
T: That's right. [E] . . . Tell me some things that happened in *Mr. Popper's Penguins* and we'll put them in sequence. [I]
S: He paints. [R]
T: OK. That's one event. . . . [E]
S: The guy was walking on the roof. [R]

T: OK, [E] do we know who? Does it give his name? [I]

S: No. He's the tightrope walker. [R]

T: Thank you James. . . . [E]

S: Captain Cook built a nest. [R]

T: OK. Very good. [E] What is it called when a penguin builds a
    nest? [I]

This sequence is very controlling for a couple of reasons. First, the underlying premise is that the teacher already knows what needs to be known and therefore takes the role of judging the quality of the student's response, positioning the teacher in the role of authority and knowledge giver and the student as the knowledge receiver without authority. Second, the IRE might better have been called a QRE since the initiating language is almost always a question. Questions exert even more control by not only insisting on a response, but also by specifying the topic of the conversation, and often the form of the response. Questions that have, or suggest, right/wrong answers exert further control by constraining not only the topic, but the range of response. This sequence offers an implicit answer to the questions posed above by Parker Palmer: knowledge is composed of facts possessed by teachers, who have the authority to transmit it to children, and children know about the world only through the knowledge that is transmitted to them. Gordon Wells calls this view of knowledge and communication "transmissionary" (Wells 2001).

There are alternatives to this epistemology in which children play a more active role in the ownership and construction of knowledge. As Barbara Rogoff and Chikako Toma (1997) point out, "Learning to act as a recipient of information and to display receipt of the information . . . [is not the same as] building on ideas in a shared endeavor [in which] participants' roles can vary widely, such as leading a shared inquiry, playing around with an idea together, or closely following other people's lines of thought" (p. 475). The following examples of talk lead to conversations, the (unspoken) premise of which is that the students are experienced thinkers who have something to say that is worth listening to. These conversational pivots are, I believe, invitations to a more productive epistemology (Johnston, Jiron, and Day 2001).

❖ ***"Let's see if I've got this right" (then summarizes students'
extended comments).***

54

By reflecting to the students their comments, the teacher at once validates their voice, shows that she is listening, and opens the possibility for them to reflect on, modify, or challenge what has been said. Unless intonation says otherwise, this takes the evaluation aspect out of the teacher's role. Another version of this comment is "Let's hold up for a moment and see where we are." While accomplishing the same thing, this one casts the teacher not so much as a listening other, but as a community member helping the community strategically manage its inquiry process. It does this by shifting from "I" to "we."

❖ "Any questions? Let's start with these." (Teacher writes them on a chart).

The effect of soliciting *student* questions is to cede control of the topic of conversation to the students, or at least to engage in more balanced negotiation of the topic—provided the questions are taken seriously and followed up on. The questions then become matters of inquiry that have further important properties (see Lindfors 1999). Among other things, they suggest a very different role of the student in the production of knowledge. They also change the students' conception of what school is about and its relation to their own personal interests. When students have listed a substantial number of questions, they can decide which ones are the most important to pursue. The result is that they become increasingly good at asking interesting questions (Comeyras 1995), particularly if they are encouraged to analyze them. For example, one teacher names a particular kind of question: "So, if you asked those questions of anyone in the class, they would have something to say on that? They're big questions." The ability or tendency to ask effective questions contributes a great deal to children's agency, and to their development of critical literacy. Dialogical contexts are particularly good for developing this ability, especially when children can ask each other questions while inquiring into something and when it is normal for questions to build on or challenge others' questions (Burbules 1993).

This is not as easy as it sounds. Because of the epistemologies in which most of us were schooled, many of us find ourselves compelled to answer students' questions when we know the answers—which we feel we should. Indeed, sometimes if we don't answer them, the students are outraged by our violation of what they thought was a clear contract. When we do answer the students' questions, we seize the authority in a way that positions students again in the less powerful position and traps them in a monologic discourse. We still have the IR (Initiate, Respond), except that the students initiate and we respond. The catch is that because of the power differential between teacher and student, the students are prevented from evaluating our responses (at least publicly). In spite of these problems, students often insist, because of their experience of being in school, that their teacher take up the monologic position of sole authority. They know how school is supposed to be done, and staying within the comfortable role, even if oppressive, is easier—like staying in an abusive (but predictable) relationship.

✣ (Silence).

Sometimes called "wait time," the attentive silence after a child's comment might better be called "thinking time." In most classrooms teachers do most of the talking, and thinking time is minimal. A teacher choosing to wait is unusual (Dillon 1988; Nystrand et al. 1997). On the face of it, remaining silent seems quite trivial, but research shows that extending thinking times is positively related to more student talk, more sustained talk, and more "higher order" thinking (see Carlsen 1991; Honea 1982; Fagan, Hassler, and Szabl 1981). Indeed, sometimes teachers deliberately slow conversation down and foreground the "thinking" part to develop more reflective habits. For example, when her students had arrived at a solution to a problem, Joan Backer asked them how they could check and then said, "Just digest that question for a minute . . . [long pause]" (Johnston and Backer 2002, p. 50).

When a teacher waits, she is not taking the floor. In a one-to-one conference it can be the same as saying, "Can you say more about that?," a phrase that such teachers also use. The overall message is something like, "I am interested in what you have to say," which positions the child as having authority. This invites identity development that includes, "I am a person whose experience and knowledge matter." Thinking time also offers respect—a relational property that is the lifeblood of a learning community. When a teacher waits for a child to figure something out or self-correct, it conveys the message that she expects the child to be able to accomplish it. Failure to wait conveys the opposite message.

In a group, thinking time can invite someone else to take the floor, with the same effect. Thinking time changes the conventional IRE to IR to seek a more extended response on the part of the student or a new response from a different student (depending on mediating nonverbal cues such as direction of gaze). This opens the possibility of shifting from IRE to IRR or, in some classrooms IRRRRRRRR, with the "I" not necessarily being provided by the teacher. As we shall see, the IRR is a more productive mode of interaction for a number of reasons.

❖ *"Thanks for straightening me out" (Adams 1995, p. 137).*

This comment from a teacher to a student implies something about the power differential between them and the epistemology in operation (or possibly the initial naiveté of the student). The comment implies that a student has done what in most classes would be unthinkable: evaluated the teacher's comments. This teacher's response, however, tells the child that not only is this acceptable in this classroom, but that helping others correct misconceptions is something to be encouraged. The response at once asserts the authority of the child in the discourse, the fallibility of the teacher, and that both are *engaged in the same intellectual project* so that preventing miscommunications and correcting errors are joint concerns. This joint intellectual adventure is the central concept of a community of inquiry. Another teacher made this clear in her response to a student's question: "I really don't know. I have no idea. Let's find out because . . . you know what, I'm interested to find out myself" (Johnston and Quinlan 2002, p. 133). For many of us, it is hard to say to the students that we don't have the answer; however, this response is powerful. It reasserts the common ("let's") intellectual project, positioning the student in an active role, and strengthens the motive for researching the question particularly by affirming the significance of the question. It simultaneously increases the likelihood of the student asking more questions and opens the possibility of exploring the question, "How can we research this question?"

❖ *"That's a very interesting way of looking at it. I hadn't thought about it that way. I'll have to think about it some more" (Johnston and Backer 2002, p. 42).*

I need to give some context for the significance of this comment. The class was discussing a book early in the year, and a marginal student made a comment that appeared to come from "left field," or possibly the galaxy beyond that. His teacher looked thoughtful and then said, "That's a very interesting way of looking at it. I hadn't thought about it that way. I'll have to think about it some more." The epistemological view communicated to the student is "I don't expect everyone to think about this

57

in the same way. I respect you and what you have to say. Keep offering possibilities because I expect to learn from them." It asserts to the class that the teacher does not have all the answers, that perspectives are bound to vary, that stretching to understand different perspectives is expected and valued, and that students (including ones whose views are different from that of the teacher) have important things to say.

In the most practical terms, the comment acts to keep the student in the conversation. Failure to accomplish this would make the teacher's job, with that student, very difficult indeed. In my view, comments like this one, in situations that would make many teachers uncomfortable, reveal real teaching genius, particularly because the teacher is not faking it. She genuinely believes she will learn from the student.

❁ "How did you know?"

This question follows a pupil's assertion of some knowledge, such as a word spelling, a fact, or an identification. It invites a narrative about the production of knowledge, checking warrants (sources of evidence or authority), and theorizing. The question assumes an intelligent attempt or comment, even if the student attempt was, in fact, not quite correct. In this way it is similar to asking, "How would someone arrive at that answer [position, or something else]?" It assumes a knowledgeable, thinking person, even though, on this occasion, he or she might not have been quite correct or successful. It is this assumption of a knowledgeable and agentive person that is the important message—the more powerful because it is not overtly stated and therefore not open to contestation. The question also turns the emphasis toward *knowing* rather than *knowledge*. Taking seriously how people know what they presume to know is an important aspect of critical literacy.

❁ "How could we check?"

This question, a close relative of the previous one, can appear at the level of figuring out a word while reading or writing, or examining social studies, literature, political statements, or a hypothesis or theory in science. The productive epistemology represented by this family of questions and comments (such as, "How could we be sure?" "What makes you think that?") is one that places children in agentive roles with respect to knowledge production, with all of the rights and responsibilities that confers.

The responsibility means that children must cross-check their sources and warrants. They begin to ask themselves these questions and expect to ask them with and of others. They require the student to use sources of information or logic to boost confidence in their construction of knowledge rather than having to seek verification from an outside authority. In some of these comments, the teacher has used the word "we" ("How could we check?") to move the burden of justification to the group rather than the individual. This prevents the individual offering the knowledge from being publicly unable to accomplish the task, while including her in the invitation to do so. As students offer possibilities and the group collectively thinks through the problem, the individual can acquire the thinking process of the group, a point explored more fully in Chapter 7.

❖ "Would you agree with that?"

On the occasion this question was offered, it invited public disagreement or at least the need to seek further information on a topic. Understanding that it is acceptable, indeed normal, to disagree, and that people have legitimate opinions that differ, is necessary for participating in a democratic society. It is also a good way to set up the public need to articulate the logic of one's position. As one student articulates her logic, it makes overt her thinking so that others can try it on. And the thinking is carried out in the context of a real and relevant problem, and made increasingly complex as difference produces a refining of logic. This develops children's critical literacy by increasing their social imagination—in this case their ability to imagine the intentions and logic of other social beings, something they will bring to their reading and their writing, if we encourage them to do so.

❖ "Is that an observation or conjecture?" (Johnston and Backer 2002, p. 47).

This question came during a week in which science studies and various other aspects of class life revolved around the birth of ducklings in the classroom. Children were routinely taking turns observing and documenting the behavior and development of the ducklings. The question asks the students to distinguish between observation and inference, to attend to the relationship between warrants and claims. It also points out to them the human tendency to add extra layers of meaning to observation. As Deanna Kuhn and her colleagues observe, "By the end of the first year of life, infants have begun to make causal inferences based on the juxtaposition of an antecedent and an outcome . . . it is the fact that this inference strategy is overlearned that causes problems" (Kuhn et al. 1995, p. 15). The question also asks students to attend to their (and others') use of language. These are central aspects of critical literacy.

❖ **"Never *believe everything I say. Never believe everything* any *adult says" (Wharton-McDonald and Williamson 2002, p. 82).***
This comment confirms that *nobody* has a corner on truth and that authority should always be questioned, checked, and warrants sought. This is another central component of the critical literacy aspect of epistemology. It normalizes human fallibility and asserts that no authority is above error, no matter how well intentioned or authoritatively positioned. More than that, though, children in such classrooms are not forced into the epistemic role of merely remembering the knowledge that has been communicated to them by teachers and texts. They learn that language is not simply a vehicle for communicating information. Children in these classrooms do not deny the communicative function of language, but view the multiple sources of language in the classroom—teacher, books, Internet, students, and their own language—as tools for thinking (Nystrand et al. 1997; Wertsch, Tulviste, and Hagstrom 1993).

I do not mean to imply here that these teachers never lecture or never engage in brief IRE sequences. Clear, explicit telling certainly has its place. In writing this book, I asked colleagues for commentaries on drafts. I sought and received the occasional mini-lecture or its print equivalent (in books and articles). These instances of people "delivering information" did not interfere with my sense that I was inquiring into the meanings of what teachers say in classrooms or eliminate my sense that I was working on an "improvable object" (Wells 1998, 2001). There are many things for me to understand if I am to advance my thinking about teaching. I will use all the help I can get. Just because I am inquiring does not mean that I have to learn everything from scratch. But finding productive ways to ask will become more important than current schooling practices suggest (Lindfors 1999), and the skill of my colleagues in deciding how much to tell and how to tell it should also not be underestimated. Learning these skills requires a community in which they are routinely practiced.

Extension

If you would like to shift the conversations in your classroom in the direction I have described, begin by planning ways to get children into open public conversations.

1. Analyze the following interaction from Debbie Miller's classroom (Miller 2002b). Notice the ways in which she positions the students with respect to each other, herself, and the subject they are studying, and how she extends their sense of agency. Consider any other comments you might add, or what you might do differently.

    DM: Oh, you guys, look at all this new learning. What's
         going on? Can you talk to me about what you've been doing?
    S1: Well, we learned a lot.
    DM: Well, tell me some of the things you've learned.
    S1: Well, I learned that the ocean has layers.
    S2: Yeah.
    DM: So what does that mean it has layers?
    S1: Like, you know what in the rain forest has layers? Well, it's
         just like it except in the rain forest it has more layers than . . .
         this only has three . . . three.
    S2: Yeah, three.
    DM: So you mean like in the ocean there's a top layer, is that how
         it goes? And then a middle layer . . .
    S1: and a bottom layer.
    DM: Wow.
    S2: Yeah, and I learned that the twilight layer . . . zone . . . is the
         middle layer.
    DM: Yeah.
    S2: It is 1,000 meters below.
    DM: Below where?
    S2: The surface.
    DM: Oh, the surface. Perfect.
    [*After further discussion*]
    DM: It's so interesting. I'm learning so much just sitting here. I
         better let you guys get back to work. Thank you for teaching
         me about those kinds of fish. And is the rest of your plan just
         to keep reading and recording?

S1: Yeah. You see this one?

DM: Keep going. You guys are doing great.

2. Next time you are reading aloud to the students, ask no questions and begin a pattern of annotating and pausing. At interesting points, say "Wow," and pause expectantly, or say, "I wonder if [some possibility] . . ." and pause. Most of all, if anyone says anything, show interest—"Oh, interesting . . . [with enthusiasm]"—then pause. Under no circumstances offer any hint of judgment—"good," "right," "yes," and so forth. Offer a relevant comment such as, "I've felt like that before . . . [pause]." When you do ask questions, make them wide open, such as, "Anyone else had that sort of feeling [experience]?" The rules of engagement for you include not judging any responses and providing ample thinking time. If pausing for longer than a breath is difficult for you, try counting slowly in your head to five—or ten—before picking up where you left off.

3. Get a conversation going in which you are not likely to be at the center. Marg Wells (Department of Education Training and Employment 2000) used the following strategy with second graders. First, they conducted a survey in the class, asking their concerns about their lives in and out of school, about their neighborhoods and the world. In that context, they asked what made the children worried, angry, or happy, and what they would like to change. From this came topics that were relevant and engaging for the children and that brought multiple perspectives and commitment.

4. Get the children to ask questions about a book you have read with them. Encourage as many as possible and write them on chart paper. Censor none. Read them all back, commenting on what an interesting collection of questions they have, and telling them that because they obviously won't have time to find answers to all of them, perhaps they could select three to answer or think through either as a class or in small (diverse) groups with their own selections. Once they can do that, you can get a little fancy by getting them to ask questions addressed to the author, such as what they would like to know that was not in the text.

5. With older students, if only some are prepared to tackle issues in book discussions, write a controversial position sentence on the board and see who agrees or disagrees. For example, if the class

has read *Puss in Boots,* the statement might be "In this book, Puss lies to everyone and even murders someone all for his own benefit. He is not the 'good guy.'" If they are reluctant to take a position, ask them to go and stand by the position (yea or nay) by which they are most persuaded, understanding that as the class discusses it, they can change their position. In science, they might do this with predictions and then discuss how they might establish credibility for their positions.

CHAPTER SEVEN

An Evolutionary, Democratic Learning Community

Democracy is neither a possession nor a guaranteed achieve-
ment. It is forever in the making; it might be thought of as a
possibility—moral and imaginative possibility. For surely it
has to do with the way persons attend to one another, care
for one another, and interact with one another. It has to do
with choices and alternatives, with the capacity to look at
things as though they could be otherwise.

GREENE 1985, P. 3

Citizens in a democracy have the convictions and enthusi-
asms of their own responses, yet they are willing to keep an
open mind about alternate points of view, and finally are
able to negotiate meanings and actions that respect both
individual diversity and community needs.

    To overcome our tendency to follow authority blindly,
we need to develop confidence in our own ability to interpret
and judge what we observe around us in the world. But con-

64

*fident and outspoken individuals must be complemented by
a tradition of conduct for reconciling differences among their
responses.*

PRADL 1996, PP. 11–12

Recall that "children grow into the intellectual life around them" and that that intellectual life is fundamentally social. The social relationships within which they learn are a part of their learning. Children, just like adults, learn better in a supportive environment in which they can risk trying out new strategies and concepts and stretching themselves intellectually. This is not just because a supportive community enables individuals to extend their minds beyond themselves without risk, but also because the relationship associated with the learning is an inextricable part of what is learned. And learning communities are not simply about being supportive. For them to be evolutionary, they also require challenge, not as a contest for power, but to "help each other and check each other's tendencies to purely idiosyncratic or self-interested thinking" (Young 1992, p. 8).

Some teachers are particularly good at building learning communities in which individuals feel valued and supported, and that sustain productive and critical learning. Children must have the experience of such communities if they are to know what to aim for in constructing their own learning environments. Students in British and American schools have limited histories in this regard. Even when they work in groups, they rarely work *as* a group, sharing ideas and working toward a common goal (Tsuchida and Lewis 1996, cited in Rogoff and Toma 1997). Because we tend to internalize the kinds of conversations in which we become involved, we should think seriously about the nature of these school interactions and their implications. The bottom line is that we need to understand how to construct or become involved in learning communities so that we extend our own development.

The comments in this chapter show how teachers use language to build caring and respectful learning communities, communities that are playful, but in which participants take each other's ideas seriously in the process of getting things done. A basic property of such communities is that they have some shared understanding of the situation and activity in which they are jointly engaged. This does not mean that they all agree, but they agree to try to understand each other to become mutually involved. They essentially agree to be parts of the same social mind for a period of time. We want communities that provide democratic and evolutionary intellectual environments (Rogoff and Toma 1997; Young 1992).

❁ "We."

To the extent that the students agree to be included in this invitation to join the classroom community, "we" is an invitation to and expression of solidarity or affinity. Teachers using collective pronouns in their interactions encourage collective stories in the students. For example, asking, "Where are we in this?" invites the response, "*We*'re agreed on the supplies we need and *we*'re about to send the fax." Of course it helps to actually have community projects in which everyone is involved—or at least groups of people are. Joint activity around shared goals produces not only the ability and desire to collaborate, but also a tacit understanding that doing so is normal. Connecting children's feelings to effective group processes along the way helps ensure that they actually seek such processes, at the same time placing themselves in potential learning situations.

❁ "Who else would like that book?"

This is an example of a family of invitations to social imagination. The idea is that to respond sensibly to such a request, one must understand other people's interests and capabilities. The unspoken assumption is that it is normal to talk with others about their books and their interests. At the same time, knowing more about one another in these ways makes it harder to be mean to one another. In classrooms that encourage this shared knowledge, children appear able to figure into their book recommendations both interest and level of competence without using relative competence as a bludgeon. Beyond that, as one student pointed out when asked who else would like the book, "Probably Patrick. . . . He's, he's not the kind of guy who laughs, and he doesn't smile too much. And in this book, he might smile" (Allington and Johnston 2002, p. 201).

Reading and writing, it turns out, are natural venues for learning about others, and some teachers use them for this purpose. Early in the school year June Williamson explains to her students, "We're doing biographies at the beginning of the year partially because it goes with what we're doing—getting to know each other and getting to know ourselves a little better" (Wharton-McDonald and Williamson 2002, p. 80). Similarly, discussions of books can lead to greater shared understanding and affiliation, and a sense of caring.

❖ *"How do you think she feels about that?"*

This question comes up both in the daily management of classroom life and in discussions of narrative fiction. Indeed, making the connection between the two is useful. During classroom altercations, we ask how the participants in the dispute feel and why. We insist that students imagine themselves in the other's shoes, taking responsibility for the effects of their own actions on others—again, a central piece of agency and democratic living. At the same time, we are building the social imagination necessary for children not only to comprehend the stories they read, but also to imagine the effect of their writing on audiences and to imagine why authors do what they do, thus enabling critical readings of others' writing.

Developing children's social imaginations in this way also allows them to see that stories are told from a perspective and that other perspectives are not equally represented. A teacher might say, for example, "You know who I would like to hear from? I want to hear what Pauline [character] thinks." Inviting children to collaboratively retell stories through assigned characters and inviting them to tell how they feel and what they think at particular points in their telling is another way of expanding this aspect of development.

Relationships among these aspects of development are complex and little understood. For example, children's social imagination is associated with their sense of well-being (Eder 1994). Stories told by children aged three to eight who have a solid sense of well-being contain more empathy and affiliation than do stories told by children with a weaker sense of well-being. These are not normally picked up on standardized accountability tests, and the causal relationships remain unclear, but if there is a chance that such side benefits are to be had—at no obvious cost—I say let's go for them. Understanding ourselves entails understanding others and how we are alike and not alike. This requires building an expansive social imagination so that we can readily see others in ourselves and ourselves in others. In the long run, the more we are able to orchestrate interactions in ways that allow us to think beyond ourselves and through each other, the more we evolve as a society and as individuals.

❧ *"Any compliments?" (Johnston and Quinlan 2002, p. 126).*
Mary Ellen Quinlan asks this unusual question of her fourth-grade students at odd transition moments, inviting them to say positive things about each other. It is part of a larger conversation she naturalizes in her classroom about personal goals and ways of relating to others. It has the effect of encouraging students to notice positive features of each other's behavior. But it is more than that. Her students initially don't really know what she means. They quickly catch on, though, and begin to notice who could *use* a compliment. This latter shift happens because she has also made it normal in her classroom to discuss what students are working on and how they feel. A student might be working on being more involved in group discussions, or on staying focused for longer periods of time, or on reading more books, for example.

❧ *"You guys say such important things, it amazes me you would talk while others are talking."*
Joan Backer made this comment during a class discussion when a couple of small groups had set up splinter discussions while one of the students had the floor. It at once drew students' attention to the problem (eliminating it), and reminded them of the reason they listen to each other and the respect that normally characterizes the community. A more positive though less informative side of this comment is demonstrated in the collective praise, "I love the way you're really listening to one another."

❧ *"I wonder . . ."*
"I wonder . . ." represents a class of linguistic lubricants. It marks the offering of a possible hypothesis, or a tentative idea with an invitation, but not an insistence, to pick it up and improve it or take it further. For group discussions to take place, such lubricants, or "tentativeness markers" (Feldman and Wertsch 1976) are necessary. Other examples include "maybe," "seems like," "perhaps," "or something," "I think," and so forth. The word "wonder" also can be a marker for a particular form of talk and possibility—what Neil Mercer (2000) calls "exploratory talk." Exploratory talk brings multiple minds together to work on the same problem in the most powerful ways.

Ensuring this kind of talk in classrooms takes conviction. Because it takes a real commitment in time, a teacher has to believe that important things come of it. They do. This experience of "thinking together" or "distributed thinking" is an example of what Mercer calls an "intermental development zone" or IDZ—a more social framing of Vygotsky's zone of proximal development (ZPD). This is where the collective intellect in which a student is participating manages to accomplish things that the solitary intellect cannot, and in the process and over time, makes it possible for the individual intellect to accomplish the same complexity of thought. The IDZ concept has an advantage over the usual interpretation of the ZPD in that the process is nonhierarchical. It is not a matter of a more advanced "other," who can already accomplish something, building a scaffold up which the less advanced learner climbs; rather, it is a process in which mutual participation produces development without the associated asymmetrical positioning.

Knowing how to participate in and to generate such interactions is a skill that, although not valued in school accountability systems, is very highly valued in the professional world. The paradox of this sort of interaction is nicely explained by Pablo del Rio and Amelia Alvarez (Rio and Alvarez 2002, pp. 68-69), who argue that

> Human abilities are based on the reconstruction of animal abilities, by extending our social and instrumental biological capacity with the help of social and cultural mediations. In the process, the helplessness that obliges humans to depend on others has turned into an exceptional ability for functional cooperation and distributed intelligence: our abilities are in origin "shared disabilities." . . . Thus, this extensive need for external mediation, social and instrumental, should not be seen as weakness—only accepted provisionally in children—but as a powerful mechanism of cultural activity and development.

❖ "Are there any other ways to think about that? Any other opinions?"

According to published research, this sort of invitation does not happen often in school. Few classrooms in the United States entertain or encourage conflicting viewpoints (Cazden 2001; Nystrand et al. 1997). We simply don't ask children to agree or disagree with each other or elaborate on each other's ideas in discussions—to use "other students' statements as thinking devices" (Tsuchida and Lewis 1996, cited in Rogoff and Toma 1997, p. 484). This is a great loss, because doing so has many benefits. First, it encourages students to seek and articulate warrants and logic for their positions. This makes their thinking available as part of the intellectual environment within which children's development occurs, and provides a motive to take on multiple lines of logic. Taking on the search for warrants and logic builds independence.

Second, the conceptual conflicts likely to arise make it possible for children to change and expand their conceptual development. Cognitive change takes place when learners must confront and coordinate conflicting viewpoints, and as they resolve the conflicts, children participate in their own development (Doise and Mugny 1984; Schaffer 1996). Disagreement, more than agreement, moves children's thinking forward (Miller 1986). Third, in experiencing their own conceptual growth in such learning situations children start to learn that difference is actually beneficial to them personally, especially if we help them notice this as it is happening. This understanding is more powerful than the concept of tolerance. Tolerance requires a degree of maintenance since it is not obviously in the individual's self-interest.

Fourth, the practice of encouraging the engagement of multiple perspectives is essentially demanded by a democratic society (Barber 1984; Burbules 1993), and therefore demanded in preparation for participation in a democratic society. Normalizing the concept that there are multiple possibilities, and that alternative perspectives frequently help us arrive at a better, more nuanced understanding of the focus of our inquiry, or a more elegant solution to a problem, is a big deal. Different perspectives help us flesh out and articulate our own position more fully. Children who are used to this sort of invitation, and thus engage in dialogue, use words such as *because, if,* and *why* more often than students who are not used to engaging in dialogue (Mercer 2000). It turns out that thinking, as opposed to imitation, requires more than two possible perspectives, interpretations, framings, or solutions.

One important function of the range of perspectives is that it expands children's social imagination (Dyson 1993), which is central to many aspects of literate development. If you can't imagine an institutional perspective or a female perspective, or an Islamic perspective, then critical reading possibilities are limited. You can't imagine how something might have been written differently, or how particular people's voices and perspectives are missing from a piece of writing. In the same way, you can't persuasively write to audiences whose perspectives you can't imagine. Neither can you convincingly construct such characters in fiction.

70

❧ *"What are you thinking? Stop and talk to your neighbor about it."*

This instruction, in the middle of a read-aloud, draws children's attention to their intellectual processes, building metacognitive awareness, and developing the capacity to share, and thus expand, those processes. At the same time, it helps children to understand that meaning-making is not a matter of getting the right answer, because they quickly learn how different people make different, yet similar, sense. In addition, the more they get to have such personal conversations with their classmates, the more they know them and the less they are able to view them through stereotypes or to put them down. Stereotype and domination are made possible by reducing the complexity of others to the handful of features that mark them as different—as not-me.

❧ *"You managed to figure that out with each other's help. How did you do that?"*

This is an invitation to tell a particular kind of narrative—a nonheroic one. In this story, there is a process (strategy or series of strategies) in which a problem is solved because people collaborated. Rehearsing the collaborative process emplots students in relationships that make them admirable for different kinds of contribution, the nature of which can be reviewed by the teacher after the telling. Indeed, often, as the teacher helps co-construct the narrative, these different contributions are prompted. This kind of narrative is the narrative of democratic living. It reminds children that often they cannot accomplish things by themselves and that collectively they can have more power than individually. For critical social action, this is very important learning. The class is learning how to use and manage the social and intellectual space they inhabit.

❧ *"I notice, Laurel, that when he was talking it sort of jogged your mind—what were you thinking?" (Johnston 1999, p. 35).*

This observation-question could be from the same classroom conversation as the previous comment because it, too, turns children's attention to the significance of group processes. Indeed, rather than inviting a narrative of joint agency, it tells one. It is the same conversation, then, even if from a different classroom. It occurred during a discussion in which the teacher was playing primarily a monitoring role. One child had the floor and was clarifying a point when a second, Laurel, said, "Oh. Oh . . ." and raised her hand to speak. In inviting her to speak, the teacher pointed out to her (and the assembled group) the significance of others' ideas for one's own thinking. There was other evidence in this class that the students became aware of this. I recorded examples of children taking extra time and effort to understand unusual comments by peers—observations that would have been ignored or scorned in many classrooms. These interactions suggested to me that, consistent with their teacher's invitation, these children had come to value different perspectives as a resource for their own learning. As a foundation for social relations, this understanding beats "tolerance" hands down. Tolerance is about resisting an assumed individual tendency to judge difference negatively, and is often simply a part of indifference. By contrast, this classroom conversation assumes that difference is a valuable resource for individual development.

❖ *"You know, Sheila, that just gave me a memory. Thank you. I'll just write it down." (Students wait while she writes).*
This comment, which occurred during a class discussion prior to writing, has several interesting features. First, as with the previous comment, it demonstrates a way in which others' contributions can be beneficial to one's own thinking—even if one is a teacher. It also clearly asserts the value of what Sheila has to say, addressing her by name, thus putting her in a powerful position. The teacher emphasizes this, providing evidence of significance, by making a written record. At the same time, it shows that a comment may be valuable in more ways than by simply adding new information. A comment can be valuable because it makes people remember things they otherwise might not have.

❖ *"How do you know when a conversation is finished?"*
This particular question came about when a book discussion group had deteriorated into something less than that, and somewhat disruptive. The teacher went over to the group and rather than reprimanding them, asked what the problem was. She received several simultaneous answers. She said, "It sounds as though you are having difficulty figuring out when a conversation is finished. How do you decide a conversation is finished?" She added that perhaps they could think through the process of their discussion group by tape-recording it the next day and doing some analysis. These were fourth graders, mind you. It is this

learning about how to manage not just one's own cognition, but the source of one's cognition in the learning environment that makes these conversations "evolutionary" (Young 1992). To oversimplify a tad, it is like learning how to manage not only the computer, but the computer networks and the people using them for your own development. Because doing so requires understanding how to approach and manage difference not only in morally productive ways, but also in ways that are mutually sustaining, this sort of process is evolutionary in terms of democratic living.

✣ *"This is how you go about making a large decision with a lot of parts. You take it in parts. Discussion is now open on how to decide which ones" (Johnston and Backer 2002, p. 49).* The fourth graders had just spent some time debating the ethics of dissecting duck eggs that were past gestation—a discussion that turned out to be a complex moral dilemma parallel in complexity to the debates on abortion. However, the discussion had reached a point of no progress. Joan broke the decision down into a sequence of separate decisions on chart paper and explained the process, providing an example of explicit strategy instruction. After brief discussion of each part, the children were able to come to almost unanimous decisions on each. I have been in many meetings in which adults are unfamiliar with this sort of social intellect management. Though such skills do not appear on any of the high-stakes tests, they are of considerable social and even economic value.

Democratic living is about social problem-solving. Indeed, we can think of education in terms of efforts to increase learner's' problem-solving ability (Clay 1991; Dewey 1985; Freire and Macedo 1987). No, the double apostrophe is not an error. Writing the sentence put me in a bind over where to put the apostrophe for two reasons. First, more of our problem-solving is social than individual, and second, becoming more accomplished at individual problem-solving requires the ability to profit from and internalize collaborative problem-solving. It is this ability of individuals to use the social to leap-frog their individual problem-solving ability *and* the ability of collections of such individuals to leap-frog their collective problem-solving ability that makes education evolutionary.

As individuals we can evolve only within the limits of our social environment and the discursive tools it offers us. Evolving as a society requires that we as individuals become able to use the social tools available to us to expand those limits. As adults, we must be able to use distributed thinking to overcome the limitations of our own experience and logic. We must learn to use the diversity of experience and perspective and intellectual resources to solve the problems that arise in democratic living, but also to ratchet forward our own intellectual development. Children entering adulthood already apprenticed into these ways of knowing and being will certainly be sought after by both private- and public-sector employers. Peter Senge (1994) has described what he calls "learning organizations," arguing that not just individuals, but organizations must be set up to learn. But, of course, the two are not independent of each other.

More important, we live in a democracy, and "strong democracy" (Barber 1984) requires that we have a learning society. As James Bovard puts it, "Democracy must be more than two wolves and a sheep voting on what to have for dinner" (Bovard 2003, p. 10). It is not enough to vote. We must participate in collectively generating the most productive solutions to social problems, with the understanding that we will disagree, and that the disagreement can extend us to possibilities we could not have imagined. I am confident that before leaving elementary school, children from some classrooms have achieved this sense of agency and the *expectation* that they will be involved in such conversations. To the extent that they (and we) see education as not being about simply gaining more knowledge, but about increasing their ability to formulate and solve meaningful problems, we will accomplish this end and reduce the chasm between education and life. They must be prepared to have better conversations about education and life than we currently have. That is what it means to have an evolutionary, indeed a democratic society.

Extension

Developing our teaching practice on our own is certainly possible. We can tape-record ourselves and listen to our language through the framework of books like this. We can interview students, listen to what they have to say, and think through its roots in our teaching talk. However, building our own learning communities is a much more productive way to go about it, and much more enjoyable. Although Vygotsky did not say this, I am sure he would have argued that, like children, teachers grow into the intellectual life around them. I'll call this Johnston's corollary to Vygotsky. All of the language and logic in this book applies as much to teachers as to students. Just like children, we have to exercise some control over that intellectual environment so that we continue to develop. This requires that we build productive learning communities, with language that reflects the dimensions we have explored in this book. It also requires engaging in open activities—ones that do not have a single path to a single solution and that allow students multiple points of entry—that require us to articulate our thinking. Now that you have a sense of the dimensions of classroom talk, let's bring them together to think through what children have to say. In Chapter 3, you considered an abstract of a conversation with Mandy. I have included in Appendix B abstracts of conversations with one of Mandy's classmates and two students from another classroom. With a couple of colleagues, read these abstracts and do the activities below.

Read the four mini-cases in Appendix B, and do the following:

1. Decide which students are from the same classroom, articulating your logic for each other as you do so. Line by line, imagine what each teacher says that makes it possible for the students to say what they do.

2. In normative terms, one student in each classroom is more competent than the other. Decide which is which, again articulating your logic.

Who Do You Think You're Talking To?

If we live, we stand in language.
You must change your words.
KENDRICK SMITHYMAN (P. 27, IN McQUEEN AND WEDDE 1985)

To understand another's speech, it is not sufficient to
understand his words—
we must understand his thought. But even that is not enough—
we must also know its motivation.
No psychological analysis of an utterance is complete
until that plane is reached.
VYGOTSKY 1986, P. 253

In a short story called "Quality Time," Barbara Kingsolver introduces readers to Miriam, who finds herself unexpectedly pregnant. Miriam confesses to her sister Janice that "I haven't even worked out what I want to pass on to a child." Janice laughs.

According to Janice, parenting was three percent conscious effort and ninety-seven percent automatic pilot. "It doesn't matter what you think you're going to tell them. What matters is they're right there watching you every minute, while you let the lady with just two items go ahead of you in line, or when you lay on the horn and swear at the guy that cuts you off in traffic. There's no sense kidding yourself, what you see is what you get." (1989, p. 68)

Teaching, like parenting, is, for much of the day, automatic. I like to think that in teaching, the proportion of conscious effort is a little higher, particularly in the planning department, but thinking through what we are going to say next *as we interact* with children would mean we were not giving them our full attention and not being genuine. Children would immediately notice this—the little planning pauses in our speech such as, "That's . . . nice." To think that children would not notice these is to seriously underestimate their ability to make sense of language. So the question is, what makes it possible for teachers to say the wonderful things they say genuinely, automatically, and consistently?

I say "consistently," because when we say something, regardless of the meaning we intend, people make sense of it given the immediate situation (as they understand it), their past experience, what has been said before, what is said afterward, and so forth. Consequently, the messages we convey about noticing, identity, agency, and epistemology have to be consistent conversational threads. We can't get away with isolated words, phrases, and sentences, no matter how wonderful they might appear. We can't use them as teaching tools as if they stand alone and can be picked up and put down at will.

I raise the issue of genuineness because we speak as human beings. Our speech is inseparable from our bodies. Its tone, modulation, pitch, and so forth are affected by feelings, attitudes, and relationships. We cannot effectively use a particular kind of language if the body and other crucial indicators give conflicting messages. If we are angry with a child, or disappointed, or think he or she is learning disabled or gifted, we might not directly say it, but traces of it will be in our speech. Kingsolver's "what you see" is made up of much more than simply the words I have highlighted in this book. The pauses, coughs, sighs, frowns, postures, and so forth are all part of our language, along with the way we organize the classroom, the activities we design, the resources we make available, and so forth. All are part of the discourse of the classroom, and all interact with one another. Children make sense of language, and themselves, in the context of it all.

Of course, the consistency and genuineness I have just mentioned are aspects of the same thing. The teachers I have described as inviting a productive epistemology invited their students into interesting conversations and were genuinely interested in what they had to say. But they were more generally interested in their students, too, not just in the ideas they contributed. They made individual personal contact with them regularly as they arrived at school and during the day, learning what in their lives mattered and what could become relevant for them. Indeed, this personal contact made it easier for them to arrive at common understandings of learning situations—what is called intersubjectivity—making joint participation in intellectual problem-solving possible. These teachers also arranged for children to come to understand *each other* in ways that allowed them to build a collective intersubjectivity. Within such an "intermental space" (Mercer 2000), children can think together, building on each other's ideas and creating an intellectual space into which their minds can expand.

Who Do You Think You're Talking To?

Let me use a fairly crude illustration. When we talk to babies, our speech is comically unlike our normal speech. We raise the pitch of our voices, reduce the length of our utterances, and use lots of questions, declaratives, and deictic references (such as "That's a book"). We also become repetitive, exaggerate inflection, and use a range of attention-getting strategies. When we talk with dogs, we sound very similar. We sound similar, but not the same (Mitchell 2001). With dogs, our utterances become even shorter. We use declaratives rather than questions, our repetitions are exact rather than varied, and we don't use deictic references. We talk *similarly* to dogs and babies, because we assume that both are inattentive and limited in their capabilities and we want to gain their attention, express affection, and perhaps control their behavior. We talk *differently* to dogs than to babies because we do not expect dogs to become real conversation partners or to grow in their ability to name things and express themselves. In other words, we talk to them differently because of what we think they are and what we think we are doing with them.

You have probably had someone talk to you in a way that made you think, "Who do you think you're talking to?" or, equally, "Who do you think you are?" When this happens to us, the other person has clearly communicated, by the way they talk to us, who they think we are. We become conscious of it because who *they* think we are conflicts with who *we* think we are. In familiar situations, we have a deep sense of who we are that we have developed in interaction with others over an extended period. Most of the time, we are unaware of the process even as we take our assigned positions in this ongoing dance. The way we interact with children and arrange for them to interact shows them what kinds of people we think they are and gives them opportunities to practice being those kinds of people. We provide them with what James Gee calls an "identity kit" (1996, p. 127). Let me give you an example. A few years ago, I interviewed a fourth-grade student, Sean. Part of the interview was as follows (edited from Johnston 1999, p. 30):

> Me: If you had a pen pal in another class and you wanted to find out about him as a reader, what kind of questions would you ask?
>
> Sean: Maybe ask them what reading level you read at . . .
>
> Me: Are there different kinds of readers in your class?
>
> Sean: There's ones like the people who's not good and the people who are good . . .
>
> Me: When you are discussing as a group do you like to contribute?
>
> Sean: Not really. 'Cause I think that what Mrs. Wilson does is right. She sort of starts off easy and then she gets real hard with the questions.
>
> Me: Do you ever disagree with the other kids with those discussions?
>
> Sean: No. 'Cause they usually be right.

There is no mistaking who Sean thinks he is in this context, and he didn't make it up out of thin air. He had help from the discourse of the classroom. Notice how he feels that the way he has been positioned, and now positions himself, is perfectly normal and appropriate.

I want to stress that Sean's teacher was not mean. Quite the reverse. She was a caring person who liked Sean very much and was attentive to him, and he liked her in return. We can certainly see traces of good/not-good reader and "levels" of reader conversations. But we can also see that it is not simply the names and labels we invoke that affect children, or for that matter the love with which we embrace them, but the ways we *unwittingly* use language to position them and provide them with the means to name and maim *themselves*. I have dedicated this book to the possibility that we can *wittingly* use the same principles to do the reverse—provide children with the means and the desire to construct themselves as responsibly literate democratic citizens. However, I must emphasize that the teachers whose language we have explored in this book used that language mostly without conscious attention to it, just as Barbara Kingsolver's Janice expected they would. They can do this, in part, because of who they think they and the children are, but also because of what they think they are doing.

What Do You Think You're Doing?

In the course of our recent research, we interviewed a teacher named Pam, who explained that in her class students do their reading aloud "for me to be sure that they have truly read it . . . which in some ways isn't fair to the students who have high skills because they could be going further" (Johnston, Jiron, and Day 2001, pp. 225–226). She also noted with regard to discussing books that there are "so few that actually stay engaged . . . with the conversation, that I don't use it too often. . . . They're very good if I'm leading the discussion . . . they're not good at making choices." It is fairly easy to hear the way Pam thinks of her students. They are people who cannot be trusted or expected to read independently or to make productive choices, children who are incapable of having a conversation. Her students also come in varieties of more and less capable, and the more capable ones are those who are "good at listening, following directions, . . . following through and doing a good job." With regard to students' different understandings of books, she observes, "I'm more concerned with writing it and correcting it and making sure I explain it to them. . . . They tend to be very accepting of problems or explanations . . . they don't question too often." Pam's stance toward her students is hierarchical and separate. She makes a fairly clear I/they distinction, rather than talking about "we." She has the knowledge and expertise to deliver to the students and makes sure that she does so. She is the sole authority in the classroom, and her job is to make sure that her students get things right.

In other words, as Pam talks about her teaching, she makes clear who she thinks she is talking to, who she thinks she is, and the nature of the activity they are engaged in. She conveys all of this in her interactions with her students. To verify this, check the transcript example on pages 53–54, which came from her classroom. Pam's students like her, and her teaching helps them perform better than average on standardized tests. However, what they learn about literacy, and themselves and each other as literate individuals—concepts not represented on standardized tests—is very different from students in certain other classrooms. It is different *because* of the way Pam genuinely and consistently uses language with her students. She uses language this way because of the way she thinks of herself, her students, and what they are doing.

A teacher who has a different view of herself, her students, and what she is doing would use different language. Take Stacey, for example (Johnston, Jiron, and Day 2001, pp. 227–228). Stacey's goal is for her students to be "independent thinkers" who "question every single thing." She insists on children discussing ideas in their books and wants them to respect one another and know "that there are going to be differences of opinion but we respect them." For her, it is important that authority in the classroom is distributed so that students can become independent, not only in terms of self-management, but in terms of their learning and thinking. She wants her students to be independent and "involved in the decision making," and to "reflect . . . [on] what's working and what's not [and] what we can do to change those things that are not working." Stacey wants her students to think of reading as "an opportunity to take themselves to another place, as an opportunity to think . . . a commitment to themselves as thinkers." A successful reader in her class "looks at reading with reader's eyes in terms of reflective thinking, and then she sees it with author's eyes in terms of intentions—what did the author intend? Why?"

Listening to Stacey talk about students and what they are doing, we hear a very different view of who she thinks students are and what she thinks they are doing together. She does not view her students hierarchically, and she does not think of teaching in terms of delivery. Literacy and learning are used to do things rather than as an end in themselves. She is very clear that students have to take responsibility for their learning and the knowledge they construct and that her job is to help them do that. She does not describe students in terms of good and bad, but in terms of interests.

Are these ways of thinking evident in her teaching interactions? Absolutely. Several of the examples I have used in the earlier chapters come from Stacey's room. When she says, "So, friends, as a writer that's what decisions you have to make," it is because she believes that's what writers do and because she views the people she is talking to as writers

(Johnston, Bennett, and Cronin 2002a). Are these differences reflected in her students' views of themselves? See if you can pick from the four cases in Appendix B which ones come from Stacey's room and which ones come from Pam's. Remember to do it with a colleague and to articulate your reasoning.

Although these examples emphasize the different kinds of literacy being acquired by fourth graders, how children understand what they are doing is fundamental even very early in children's literacy careers. For example, although early instructional interventions focus overwhelmingly on children's phonological awareness, their orientation toward literacy learning situations may be even more important. Children who focus on getting praise or on not looking foolish have a much harder time becoming literate than children who focus on engagement in learning activities (Niemi and Poskiparta 2002; Poskiparta et al. 2003). These social-emotional orientations toward literacy learning are very much associated with who children think they are and what they think they are doing which, to some degree at least, reflects classroom conversations and social arrangements.

Ways of Thinking: Ways of Interacting

The point I wish to make is that these teachers have very different ways of thinking about who they are, who their students are, and what they think they are doing, and these ways of thinking strongly influence the language they use automatically. Consider first-grade teacher Debbie Miller (2002b). When Debbie says to her students as they leave at the end of the day, "Thanks for coming," she could have planned to say that in advance. Of course, the students would know whether or not she was being genuine because of the comment's consistency with the rest of the classroom discourse. However, she could not plan the following interaction, when Brendan shares with the class what happened when he read a particular nonfiction book:

> Debbie: [*To Brendan*] Can I tell the other really brilliant thing that
> you did? [*To the class*] Brendan had read this book before, but
> what he did was, he just picked it up again, right? And then,
> when he read it again, he said, "I never knew this. This is a
> poem." The first time he read it and the second time and the
> third time he was just thinking about learning the words and

82

figuring out the words, right Brendan? But then, this time, he
made this big discovery that it's actually written as a . . .
[Students fill in "poem"] and who would have thought that a
nonfiction book could actually be poetry? He learned that
today, and that's because I think he had read it before.

Brendan: And Mrs. Miller didn't know that [big smile].

Debbie: I didn't know that, and you taught that to me. It was . . . I
wrote it right down here in my notebook. Thank you, Brendan.

I assume that, by this point, you are doing your own analysis of
interactions, but just in case you are interested in my interpretation, go
to Appendix C. The main thing I would highlight is the consistency
within the interaction in terms of epistemological stance. Debbie could
not fake this interaction and the many such interactions during the day
that are consistent with it on so many levels (like the other example
from her classroom on pages 61–62), because they happen on the spot,
without planning time, and they happen over and over again. How does
she do it?

In an interview, here's how Debbie explains what she is doing when
she arranges reading discussions among the children (Miller 2002a):

I'm not concerned so much as to the content of what they're saying,
really—I mean, I'm interested in that, but I'm really interested in
"so what did you notice about yourself as a learner when you were
talking with somebody?" . . . I mean, I want to make that broader
leap. . . . What kinds of new ideas can you learn from somebody
else? Did you find out something or did you learn something that
you didn't know before? . . .

When I ask them to go eye to eye and knee to knee [to discuss],
[it] is just to give them more experience actually accessing what
they know and being able to articulate it in a way it makes sense to
somebody else and then to build on each other's thinking. And so
that's . . . you know, I think, even the bigger—the bigger idea.

What she thinks she is doing is getting children to understand that
they have something to say, and that engaging with others is in their
own developmental interests in terms of what they can learn about the
world and about themselves as learners, and the thoughts they can
entertain. She wants them to treat each other with that in mind. She

wants them to be aware of themselves as learners, and of how they actually do what they do.[1] Her language is primarily a reflection of these goals. If we want to change our words, we need to change our views.

Changing Our Words and Keeping Our Heads Up

Although the genuineness and consistency these teachers show in their interactions with students lies in these deeper beliefs, I think we can start to change our classroom interactions by changing our words and dragging some of our beliefs along with them. The language I have suggested throughout the book is likely to result in changes in other aspects of the classroom dynamic. For example, "That's like . . . ," "How else?," and "Did anyone notice . . ." are ways of starting useful conversations that can be consciously applied with little complication. Certainly, reflecting to students what they are doing well can be instituted with substantial effect and minimal additional requirements. We just have to make it a priority, and we might have to consciously edit our speech for a bit. We can also make it clear to students that we are interested in what they have to say. If you tried the exercises at the end of Chapter 6, I hope you found this to be the case.

However, making major change in our language is difficult without having other supports in place. Most important, unless what the children are doing in school is meaningful, that is, relevant to their immediate lives and goals, they will easily help us shift back into unproductive language. Indeed, many of the comments discussed in the book can be seen as vehicles for making learning meaningful to students, and students productively meaningful to themselves and each other. As Vygotsky pointed out, meaningfulness is what makes it possible for children to interact in productive ways, and to be in control of their learning, integrating the connections among thinking, acting, and feeling. Without meaningful activity, children do not develop internal control (Rio and Alvarez 2002). Yet, pressures of testing and overstuffed curricula easily make us abandon meaningfulness and reduce our view of our work to mere individual cognitive skill building. It is easy to forget

---

1. To get a full sense of consistency and genuineness of Debbie's interactions, as well as an understanding of how classroom organization and planning fit into the picture, I recommend that you check her videotapes, *Happy Reading!*

the need to engage the whole person in joint community activities that are socially and personally meaningful and emotionally satisfying.

To be meaningful, teaching children to become literate is about the here and now, and what children can do with literacy to serve their interests. However, for us, it is at least as much about the society we wish for our children and who we wish our children to become. The possibility of an evolutionary democratic society depends on children's understandings of who they are (and might become), their epistemological understandings, what they take to be normal relationships with others, and the narratives they can imagine for themselves. We can keep the tests and other potentially distracting elements in mind, but we have to keep our heads up further than that as we deal with the moment-to-moment interactions with students. In a tense, emotionally charged situation, for example, in which there is no time for planning, Tracy says to a student:

> Feelings are hurt and so because you don't deal with them, you . . . you walk away being angry, and I don't want that to happen . . . you know . . . it wasn't your intention to hurt his feelings but you were angry. I'm just trying to get you to understand why he would respond the way he did and why you would respond the way you did . . . I don't want to invalidate how you are feeling . . . just understand why you are feeling the way you do . . . then we'll all have a better understanding of one another. (Johnston, Bennett, and Cronin 2002a)

Tracy's goal is not merely to deal with the immediate situation. She has a larger goal in mind. Perhaps I should say that she is dealing with the immediate situation within a larger frame of reference—an activity and goal structure that saturate her language choices. She is addressing these cranky students within the same principles she holds for her literacy instruction. It is her belief that understanding ourselves entails understanding others and how we are alike and not alike, and our intentions, thoughts, and feelings. This, in turn, requires an expansive social imagination so that we can readily see others in ourselves and ourselves in others. In this line of thinking, the more we understand each other as extensions of ourselves, and difference as potential for our own development, the more critically literate we will be and, as Mary Rose O'Reilley would have it, the less likely we are to kill one another.

Robert Young (1992) observes that we are "entitled to ask of any view of human learning and inquiry: 'What image of humanity is inherent in it?'" I hope the contrasting examples in this chapter encourage you to do this. I hope I have also convinced you that exploring the image of humanity inherent in the language of our teaching is not merely an entitlement. It is a responsibility. I know the image I stand with. I stand with Mary Rose, Joan, Debbie, Stacey, and the many other teachers whose words I have shown you, working for a society we can *live* with. When I say "live with," I do not mean only in the sense of not being killed, but with the understanding that to live means to grow, and that failure to grow intellectually and socially is not living, but merely existing. In my view, the real beauty in these teachers' classroom talk is that they show us that teaching toward such a society does not entail compromising more narrowly academic ends. We can have our cake and eat it, too.

The Fine Print

To begin writing this book, I needed to get to the point as quickly as possible, so I took a few liberties: I swept a few details about language under the rug. By choosing to read this appendix you have lifted the rug, so I must assume that you are interested in those details, even if they are a bit messier than the tidied-up version of language I present in the rest of the book. In some ways, you might view this appendix as the fine print—the "some restrictions apply" and "void where prohibited" clauses.

Language turns out to be a very tricky tool for communication. Although I have written much of this book as if particular words and phrases have specific meanings, words by themselves mean nothing—only what the social context allows them to say. Whatever is said before, or after, will change the meaning. For example, the meaning of "good," said in response to a student's work, will be changed by saying "fantastic" to the next student.

Even saying nothing can mean different things. Although I present "wait time" in Chapter 6 as if it means one thing, its meaning depends on where it occurs in a conversation between which people. You can probably imagine a conversation in which a silence means "I don't think I believe you," another in which it means "You win," another in which it means "How dare you," and still another in which it means "You really disappointed me." Each of these will be accompanied by different body positions and facial expressions. A silence will also feel different depending on who is present and their social standing with relation to one another. In other words, to understand what someone is saying we have to make a bunch of assumptions about the circumstances: who the person thinks they are, who they think we are, what sort of interaction this is, and so forth.

Generating these shared meanings (communicating) is accomplished not only through language, but also through a range of other cultural tools such as facial expression, gesture, voice tone, and spatial arrangements. To complicate things further, each of us carries around in our bodies a history of the interactions in which we have been involved—what Pierre Bourdieu called "habitus" (Bourdieu 1977, 1990). Silence will *feel* different (mean different things) to people with different interactional histories and in different contexts. The meaning of language depends, too, on the relational context. Without trust and respect many of the examples in this book become quite unpredictable.

Children often bring very different assumptions about how adults and children interact. For example, children might come to school assuming that adults normally ask questions to which they already know the answer, or that interacting with adults is a formal event. If they encounter different patterns in school, it might take a while to sort out how home and school are different contexts. Similarly, children used to direct language might be puzzled when they encounter indirect requests such as, "Would you like to open your books now?" These examples are common cultural conflicts children experience on entering school, and there are many more. Children have different expectations about how boys and girls should interact, and there are subtle differences in socially appropriate behavior. For example, the length of time people wait to be sure that someone has finished what they are saying is much shorter in New York City, say, than in rural New York (Scollon and Scollon 1981).

As you can see, then, I am taking some liberties in assuming that the things teachers say have consistent unequivocal implications. Although I must plead guilty to this charge, I would like to offer that, within stable language communities we take a lot for granted. If we didn't we would never understand anything. In classrooms, as in any language situation, we have to have some rules, or things that we can count on. Just as in any game, if you don't know the rules, everything gets thrown into confusion and people get hurt. There are normative rules about how we interact, and there are "expected" responses. For example, when we ask a question, we expect an immediate answer. If we don't get one, we figure there must be a reason. If a teacher asks a student, "Are you okay?" and there is a pause before the response, we can assume the answer is "Not really," even if the spoken answer is "Yes." Let's say we ask a question, assuming that we will get an answer, and get "You wish!" We have to assume that, even though it is not a direct answer to the question, it nonetheless contains an answer.

At the beginning of the year in classrooms, many of the rules and relationships are up for grabs, and children (and teacher) are busy figuring out how to make common sense. The teacher has the opportunity to set up the rules and consistencies so that children know what they can count on. It will behoove us to know something about how language histories vary among cultures so that we do not take for granted the interpretations children make. In the meantime, it might be worth remembering that treating interactional problems as ones of misinterpretation is a much safer default than treating them as willful disobedience. As I suggest in this book, each person in an interaction claims to be a particular kind of person and implies that the others in the interaction are particular kinds of people. Implying that a child is a disobedient kind of person is not helpful, particularly if the child decides it is a reasonable identity to work with.

The bottom line is that in this small book, I do not really deal with the cultural and linguistic variation we encounter in classrooms. There might be some saving features, though. For example, the epistemological stance I favor throughout is one that has been presented as favorable at least for African American students (Ladson-Billings 1994) as well as more generally (Applebee 1996; Nystrand et al. 1997).

Overlaps, Common Themes, and Other Liberties

While I am in confessional mode, I should say that I have also taken some liberties with the ideas of agency and narrative presented in Chapter 4. For example, I have written as if there is only one kind of narrative. Of course, there are many. There are class, gender, and cultural differences in the ways people tell personal narratives. This can produce misunderstandings when children tell stories in class that do not fit the narrative form we expect (Michaels 1986). Sometimes we have to tune our ears to these cultural differences, perhaps using local cultural representatives such as parents to help us. However, of equal significance from my perspective are the narrative differences that lead to inequities. For example, some cultures do not pass on the same narrative possibilities to boys and girls. In school, we try to help children open possibilities by restructuring the narratives they have available. This is also part of counseling practice (Wortham 2001). If this seems like monkeying with people's cultures, it is. This is one of the many reasons why teaching is a political activity.

I have taken similar liberties with the concept of agency. What I have referred to as agency (in line with work by, Bruner 1994b; Dyson 1999; Harre 1998; Wells 1998), others have referred to as self-efficacy (Bandura 1996), sense of control, or effectance (Skinner, Zimmer-Gembeck, and Connell 1998). These concepts are not all identical, but in my view, they have more than enough in common to make this conflation reasonable. Some of my suggestions regarding agency and narrative have also come from a field called "attribution theory," which is the study of people's attributions for successful and unsuccessful experiences (Foote 1999; Licht 1993; Nicholls 1989; Nolen-Hoeksema, Girus, and Seligman 1986; Skinner et al. 1998). Though these fields are different, they overlap a great deal and address much the same thing: the stories children use to make sense of their experience.

There is actually a lot of overlap among different domains of research. Indeed, although I have separated teachers' language use into different chapters to emphasize different dimensions, the obvious overlap among categories and consequences should not surprise us. We can see this from research with younger children. For example, research into parent-child interactions tells us that children who have a greater sense of agency are likely to have experienced warm and caring home environments that emphasized independence (Grolnick and Ryan 1989, 1992; Nolen-Hoeksema et al. 1995). Children with a weaker sense of agency are more likely to have experienced critical or punitive environments (Hokoda and Fincham 1995; Wagner and Phillips 1992; Nowicki and Schneewind 1982). These sort of conclusions fit well with what I discuss in the book, and when people coming at things from different directions arrive at similar conclusions, the overlaps and consistencies offer more confidence.

I should make one final note on the term "discourse," which I use here and there in the book to refer to the broader communicative context of which talk is but one facet. The clearest, and probably most widely quoted, definition of discourse is that provided by James Gee:

> Discourses are ways of being in the world, or forms of life which integrate words, acts, values, beliefs, attitudes, and social identities,

as well as gestures, glances, body positions, and clothes. A Discourse is a sort of identity kit which comes complete with the appropriate costume and instructions on how to act, talk, and often write, so as to take on a particular social role that others will recognize. (1996, p. 127)

Gee marks this broad cultural definition of Discourse with an uppercase D, distinguishing it from the moment-to-moment, face-to-face discourse of the classroom with a lowercase d. He makes the point that discourse operates both in the immediate interactions and on the grander cultural scale and that each influences the other. This book emphasizes the immediate classroom interactions, although I do make frequent reference to aspects of the larger cultural Discourse. In Chapter 8 I describe how talk, values, beliefs, attitudes, and identities fit together; see Chapter 8 for more detail.

Four Fourth Graders

These four "cases" are adapted from "Teaching and Learning Literate Epistemologies" (Johnston, Jiron, and Day 2001)

Mandy

Mandy says that a good writer "writes fast. . . . [For example] when the teacher tells us to write a story then it doesn't even take her . . . not even ten minutes." Mandy does not talk with other students about their writing. She "wouldn't want to hurt their feelings or nothing because sometimes when someone comes up to them and says, 'Oh, you're a bad writer,' and everything. Then, they'll tell the teacher . . ." Mandy says that they should not give other students ideas, "because then that would be giving them things that you thought of in your head. . . . Then they'll have, probably, the same stories."

Good readers, she says, are "all the kids that are quiet and they just listen . . . they challenge themselves . . . they get chapter books." Asked to describe herself as a reader or a writer, she says she doesn't understand the question. She does not know how she could learn about another child as a reader or writer.

Asked whether they do research in her class, she says she is unsure what it is. When it is explained, she says they don't do it. Mandy expects on her report card an "excellent" for writing and a comment like, "Mandy has behaved and she is nice to other classmates." To help a classmate become a better reader, she would tell him or her to "stop fooling around because the more you fool around, the more you get your name on the board and checks . . . [and] . . . if he doesn't know that word, if he doesn't know how to sound it out or if he doesn't know what it means, look it up in the dictionary."

In talking about books, Mandy makes no connections across books or with personal experience (pp. 226–227).

Steven

As a writer, Steven is confident about the significance of his own experience and the experiences of others. He uses these in his writing to figure out audience and characters. He took three weeks to write one of his pieces, including "some really hard struggles" (said with relish). In a reflection about a piece of writing he says, "But then I said to myself, well, where's a place that gets the reader in good suspense so they want to read on, but it's a good stopping place?" And, "So I was looking at it and I'm like, well, how can I say that this statue, I mean that this trophy is really important to me. And how can I make it . . . make that word 'trophy' be more symbolized in the statue. And I based it on the trophy, but it was really about a statue."

What he does well as a writer is "express my feelings well" and "really get out what I want to say," but sometimes he gets "into a staring match with a blank page."

In his research on racial segregation in airports, he tried two different libraries and the Internet, and called the local airport. He has not encountered discrepant information sources yet, but if he did, he would "take those two opinions and put them together and then I would have a variety of what one author thought and what the other author thought. So I would just put them together . . . and see what I came up with . . . or perhaps try to even it out."

Asked whether there are any good authors in his class, he says, "For the funny part, Jessie is really funny. He writes a lot about fantasy stuff. . . . Ron's a pretty good writer . . . and he's a little better at drawing than writing . . . Emily [in her mystery] gave details. She described the characters. It was a really good mystery because it had a point and it had something that the reader had to figure out." He has a great deal of knowledge about the structure of different genres—realistic fiction, fantasy, mystery, and biography, among others. Commenting on his own piece, he says, "Unlike most mysteries it has a sad ending."

He routinely makes connections among the books he reads and has specific criteria for what he appreciates about particular books (p. 229).

Henry

Describing himself as a writer, Henry says he's "Typical. I don't, like, . . . finish a final copy and start writing another story right away. . . . It takes me a little longer. I write a lot of stuff that's happened to me. Like, I have entries about like when I was at the beach with my friends, or I can borrow [ideas]." The most recent thing he learned as a writer is "how to be more organized," and next he would like to learn how to write longer stories because "I have lots of information . . . I know I've got more."

Conferences with friends, he says, "give me, like, ideas to put in there . . . [or] they think it's good, it's got enough details and stuff then I could meet with the teacher." Asked whether there are different kinds of readers in his class, he says, "Like Steve, he reads longer books than other people. And Dan. When he gets into a book, you're not going to stop him, like if you say, 'Hey, Dan, listen to this sentence.' He's . . . not going to come out of that book. Jenny, she reads hard books like Steve. But, umm, she finishes books, like, really fast. . . . Priscilla. She really likes to read mysteries. She reads long stories, like Nancy Drew." He also notes that, like him, Roger enjoys the Bailey School Kids books. To learn about a pen pal as a reader, he would ask, "What kind of books do you like? Who's your favorite author? What book are you reading now? . . . Have you read any good books lately?"

To help a classmate become a better reader: "If they are reading harder books that are too hard for them, [tell them] not to push themselves as much . . . maybe later in a couple of months read those books. Push them to the side and read, like, books that are at your level."

Henry enjoys adding to class discussions of books. "Like Mrs. Hopkins says when we are in the literature group, I always have something to relate to the book." He finds other students' experiences and interpretations of the book interesting, except "If they talk about some of the really little details that you don't really need." He feels comfortable disagreeing with other students and quotes what he said to a classmate on a particular occasion. He enjoys reading, and often makes connections between books. He also thinks some of the students in the class are good authors, because, for example, when "Emelia read hers . . . it was really long, but I'm like, what's going to happen next? . . . Once you get into it you want to know what's going to happen next. Their mysteries are really a mystery." This is not always true with commercial books. "Like it says the 'Boxcar Children Mysteries' on the front of the book and it says the mystery of the missing something . . . and then, like, I can't get the mystery out of it. . . . It just doesn't give it to you."

When he encounters conflicts among books when researching a topic, he says that one of the authors "probably hadn't done his homework." His strategy for dealing with such situations is to consult more sources (pp. 228–229).

Millie

Millie chose *Superfudge* to read "because it was, like, challenging, the words that was in there. . . . Because we don't read that book until fifth grade and I was going to try it." She likes realistic fiction, though she does not have a term for describing it. She thinks that as a reader, "I'm not all perfect in reading. But I'm good. But I mess up a lot because when you mess up, you learn from your mistakes."

Asked whether there are different readers in her class, she uses a good/not-good continuum and levels: "Well, they can read more better than me because when they read, they don't mess up as much as I do . . . they are on a higher level than me." She says that she has changed as a reader "because I'm reading more and more and bigger stories than last year." What she would like to learn next is to "learn books harder than chapter books . . . so I can almost get on a higher level." She likes to add to discussions when they have them. For example, the class disagreed on whether the author of *Stone Fox* should have let Searchlight die. She never disagrees with the teacher.

Her best piece of writing she thinks took fifteen to twenty minutes, and she selected it because "We had to write what does responsibility mean and I won." Asked what she does well as a writer, she says, "People tell me that when I write, I write good because . . . I say what I want to say, not what somebody else says. I don't take people's ideas, I just think of my own and just write." The thing she learned most recently about writing is that "if you write and you copy off of somebody that means you're not . . . you're acting like you're not a real writer. 'Cause if you were a real writer, you would think of your own ideas to make your own story." Her friend is a good author because she "tells examples . . . and she makes her stories long."

To help someone with writing: "If they need help, or in spelling . . . in cursive I would give them . . . 'cause I have sheets, spelling sheets that you can trace and stuff . . . and they can practice." Asked whether they do research in her class she says, "The research we do, like if we need a word that we don't know what it means, we will look it up in a dictionary." She has never encountered conflicting sources of information (p. 227).

APPENDIX C

Analysis of Debbie Miller's Interaction with the Class and Brendan

Debbie Miller's Comments	Analysis
DM: Can I tell the other really brilliant thing that you did?	Asks student's permission to share his skill and knowledge, thus maintaining his authority. "Really brilliant" might have pointed to a less helpful stable characteristic such as "smart," but here it is associated with the strategies used, making it smart to use strategies.
Brendan had read this book before, but what he did was, he just picked it up again,	It is okay to reread books.
right?	Checking with the authority to make sure the story is accurate from his point of view, reminding the class, and Brendan, of his authority.
And then, when he read it again, he said, "I never knew this. This is a poem" . . .	When we reread, we can notice new things in part because our focus is different. One thing to notice is poetry.
The first time he read it and the second time and the third time he was just thinking about learning the words and figuring out the words,	Reading something a lot can be useful. Notice what happens in your mind when you read.
Right, Brendan?	Checking with the authority to make sure the story is accurate from his point of view, reminding the class, and Brendan, of his authority.
But then, this time, he made this big discovery that it's actually written as a . . . [poem].	Be sure to notice surprises because they are often important, new information. Pauses to invite children's participation in the reconstructed think-aloud.

. . . who would have thought that a nonfiction book could actually be poetry?	Reminder of surprise and its significance, both the immediate learning and for future possibilities.
He learned that today, and that's because I think he had read it before.	Rereading often leads to new learning.
B: And Mrs. Miller didn't know that [big smile].	Brendan recognizes his own authority, his own agency, along with the feeling of associated pride. Understands that children can teach teachers, and the underlying principle of distributed cognition.
I didn't know that, and you taught that to me.	Affirms student's successful learning and his teaching, and reaffirms that teachers don't know everything.
I wrote it right down here in my notebook.	Additional affirmation, again asserting the student's authority.
Thank you, Brendan.	One final mark of respect for the student, and of the value placed on learning.

References

Adams, E. L. 1995. A Descriptive Study of Second Graders' Conversations About Books. Ph. D diss., State University of New York–Albany.

Allington, R. L. 1980. "Teacher Interruption Behaviors During Primary Grade Oral Reading." *Journal of Educational Psychology* 72: 371–377.

———. 2002. "What I've Learned About Effective Reading Instruction from a Decade of Studying Exemplary Elementary Classroom Teachers." *Phi Delta Kappan* 83, 10/June: 740–747.

Allington, R. L., and P. H. Johnston. 2002a. "Integrated Instruction in Exemplary Fourth-Grade Classrooms." In R. L. Allington and P. H. Johnston, eds., *Reading to Learn: Lessons from Exemplary Fourth-Grade Classrooms*. New York: Guilford.

Allington, R. L., and P. H. Johnston, eds. 2002b. *Reading to Learn: Lessons from Exemplary Fourth-Grade Classrooms*. New York: Guilford.

Anderson, C. 2000. *How's It Going? A Practical Guide to Conferring with Student Writers*. Portsmouth, NH: Heinemann.

Applebee, A. N. 1996. *Curriculum as Conversation: Transforming Traditions of Teaching and Learning*. Chicago: University of Chicago Press.

Austin, J. 1962. *How to Do Things with Words*. Oxford: Clarendon Press.

Bandura, A. 1996. *Self-Efficacy: The Exercise of Control*. New York: Freeman.

Barber, B. 1984. *Strong Democracy: Participatory Politics for a New Age*. Berkeley: University of California Press.

Bateson, G. 1979. *Mind and Nature: A Necessary Unity*. New York: Dutton.

Beach, K. 1995. "Activity as a Mediator of Sociocultural Change and Individual Development: The Case of School-Work Transition." *Mind, Culture, and Activity* 2: 285–302.

Blumenfeld, P. C. 1992. "Classroom Learning and Motivation: Clarifying and Expanding Goal Theory. *Journal of Educational Psychology* 84: 272–281.

Bourdieu, P. 1990. *The Logic of Practice*. Cambridge: Polity Press.

Bovard, J. 2003. Quoted in *Funny Times*. November.

Brashares, A. 2003. *The Second Summer of the Sisterhood*. New York: Delacorte.

Bruner, J. 1986. *Actual Minds, Possible Worlds*. Cambridge, MA: Harvard University Press.

———. 1987. "Life as Narrative." *Social Research* 54, 1: 11–32.

————. 1994a. "Life as Narrative." In A. H. Dyson and C. Genishi, eds., *The Need for Story: Cultural Diversity in Classroom and Community*, pp. 28–37. Urbana, IL: National Council of Teachers of English.

————. 1994b. "The 'Remembered' Self." In U. Neisser and R. Fivush, eds., *The Remembering Self: Construction and Accuracy in the Self-Narrative*, pp. 41–54. Cambridge: Cambridge University Press.

Burbules, N. 1993. *Dialogue in Teaching: Theory and Practice.* New York: Teachers College Press.

Carlsen, W. S. 1991. "Questioning in Classrooms: A Sociolinguistic Perspective." *Review of Educational Research* 61: 157–178.

Cazden, C. B. 1992. "Revealing and Telling: The Socialization of Attention in Learning to Read and Write." *Educational Psychology* 12: 305–313.

————. 2001. *Classroom Discourse: The Language of Teaching and Learning*, 2nd ed. Portsmouth, NH: Heinemann.

Clay, M. M. 1991. *Becoming Literate: The Construction of Inner Control.* Portsmouth, NH: Heinemann.

————. 1993. *Reading Recovery: A Guidebook for Teachers in Training.* Portsmouth, NH: Heinemann.

————. 2001. *Change Over Time in Children's Literacy Development.* Portsmouth, NH: Heinemann.

Cobb, P., and J. Bowers. 1999. "Cognitive and Situated Learning Persepctives in Theory and Practice." *Educational Researcher* 28, 2: 4–15.

Comeyras, M. 1995. "What Can We Learn from Students' Questions?" *Theory into Practice* 34, 2: 101–106.

Coulthard, M. 1977. *"Conversational Analysis": An Introduction to Discourse Analysis.* London: Longman.

Davies, B., and R. Harre. 1999. "Positioning and Personhood." In R. Harre and L. v. Langenhove, eds., *Positioning Theory: Moral Contexts of Intentional Action*, pp. 32–52. Oxford: Blackwell.

Delpit, L. 1988. "The Silenced Dialogue: Power and Pedagogy in Educating Other People's Children." *Harvard Educational Review* 58, 3: 280–298.

Department of Education Training and Employment. 2000. *Social Action Through Literacy: Early to Primary Years.* Adelaide: University of South Australia.

Dewey, J. 1985. *Democracy and Education.* Carbondale: Southern Illinois University Press.

Dillon, J. T. 1988. "The Remedial Status of Student Questioning." *Curriculum Studies* 20: 197–210.

Doise, W., and G. Mugny. 1984. *The Social Development of the Intellect.* Oxford: Pergamon Press.

Donaldson, M. 1978. *Children's Minds.* New York: W. W. Norton.

Dunham, P. J., F. Dunham, and A. Curwin. 1993. "Joint-Attentional States and Lexical Acquisition at 18 Months." *Developmental Psychology* 29: 827–831.

Dyson, A. H. 1993. *Social Worlds of Children Learning to Write in an Urban Primary School.* New York: Teachers College Press.

————. 1999. "Coach Bombay's Kids Learn to Write: Children's Appropriation of Media Material for School Literacy." *Research in the Teaching of English* 33, 4: 367–402.

Dyson, A. H., and C. Genishi. 1994. "Introduction: The Need for Story." In A. H. Dyson and C. Genishi, eds., *The Need for Story: Cultural Diversity in Classroom and Community*, pp. 1–7. Urbana, IL: National Council of Teachers of English.

Eder, R. A. 1994. "Comments on Children's Self-Narratives." In U. Neisser and R. Fivush, eds., *The Remembering Self: Construction and Accuracy in the Self-Narrative*, pp. 180–190. New York: Cambridge University Press.

Elbers, E., and L. Streefland. 2000. "'Shall We Be Researchers Again?' Identity and Social Interaction in a Community of Inquiry." In H. Cowie and G. v. d. Aalsvoort, eds., *Social Interaction in Learning and Instruction: The Meaning of Discourse for the Construction of Knowledge*, pp. 35–51. Amsterdam: Pergamon Press.

Fagan, E. R., D. M. Hassler, and M. Szabl. 1981. "Evaluation of Questioning Strategies in Language Arts Instruction." *Research in the Teaching of English* 15: 267–273.

Feldman, C., and J. Wertsch. 1976. "Context Dependent Properties of Teachers' Speech." *Youth and Society* 8: 227–258.

Fennimore, Beatrice S. 2000. *Talk Matters: Refocusing the Language of Public School.* New York: Teachers College Press.

Fivush, R. 1994. "Constructing Narrative, Emotion, and Self in Parent-Child Conversations About the Past." In U. Neisser and R. Fivush, eds., *The Remembering Self: Construction and Accuracy in the Self-Narrative*, pp. 136–157. New York: Cambridge University Press.

Fletcher, Ralph. 1993. *What a Writer Needs.* Portsmouth, NH: Heinemann.

Foote, C. J. 1999. "Attribution Feedback in the Elementary Classroom." *Journal of Research in Childhood Education* 13, 3: 155–166.

Freire, P., and D. Macedo. 1987. *Literacy: Reading the Word and the World.* Hadley, MA: Bergin and Garvey.

Gauvain, Mary. 2001. "The Social Context of Cognitive Development." In C. B. Kopp and S. R. Asher, eds., *The Guilford Series on Social and Emotional Development.* New York: Guilford.

Gee, J. P. 1996. *Social Linguistics and Literacies: Ideology in Discourses*, 2nd ed. London: Falmer Press.

Graves, D. H. 1994. *A Fresh Look at Writing.* Portsmouth, NH: Heinemann.

Greene, Maxine. 1985. "The Role of Education in Democracy." *Educational Horizons* 63: 3–9.

Grice, H. P. 1975. "Logic and Conversation." In P. Cole and J. L. Morgan, eds., *Syntax and Semantics 3: Speech Acts*, pp. 41–58. New York: Academic Press.

Grolnick, W. S., and R. M. Ryan. 1989. "Parent Styles Associated with Children's Self-Regulation and Competence: A Social Contextual Perspective." *Journal of Educational Psychology* 81: 143–154.

Halliday, M. A. K. 1993. "Towards a Language-Based Theory of Learning." *Linguistics and Education* 5: 93–116.

———. 1994. *An Introducation to Functional Grammar*, 2nd ed. London: Edward Arnold.

Harre, R. 1998. *The Singular Self: An Introduction to the Psychology of Personhood.* Thousand Oaks, CA: Sage.

Harre, R., and G. Gillet. 1994. *The Discursive Mind.* Thousand Oaks, CA: Sage.

Hokoda, A., and F. D. Fincham. 1995. "Origins of Children's Helpless and Mastery Achievement Patterns in the Family." *Journal of Educational Psychology* 87: 375-385.

Honea, M. 1982. "Wait Time as an Instructional Variable: An Influence on Teacher and Student." *Clearinghouse* 56: 167–170.

Hutchby, I., and R. Wooffitt. 1997. *Conversation Analysis.* Oxford: Blackwell.

Ivey, G. 2002. "'Responsibility and Respect for Themselves and for Whatever It Is They're Doing': Learning to Be Literate in an Inclusion Classroom." In R. L. Allington and P. H. Johnston, eds., *Reading to Learn: Lessons from Exemplary Fourth-Grade Classrooms,* pp. 54–77. New York: Guilford.

Ivey, G., P. H. Johnston, and J. Cronin. 1998. *Process Talk and Children's Sense of Literate Competence and Agency.* Montreal: American Educational Research Association.

Johnston, P. H. 1999. "Unpacking Literate 'Achievement.'" In J. Gaffney and B. Askew, eds., *Stirring the Waters: A Tribute to Marie Clay.* Portsmouth, NH: Heinemann.

Johnston, P. H., S. Guice, K. Baker, J. Malone, and N. Michelson. 1995. "Assessment of Teaching and Learning in 'Literature Based' Classrooms." *Teaching and Teacher Education* 11, 4: 359–371.

Johnston, P. H., S. Layden, and S. Powers. 1999. *Children's Literate Talk and Relationships.* Montreal: American Educational Research Association.

Johnston, P. H., and J. Backer. 2002. "Inquiry and a Good Conversation: 'I Learn a Lot from Them.'" In R. L. Allington and P. H. Johnston, eds., *Reading to Learn: Lessons from Exemplary Fourth-Grade Classrooms,* pp. 37–53. New York: Guilford.

Johnston, P. H., T. Bennett, and J. Cronin. 2002a. "'I Want Students Who Are Thinkers.'" In R. L. Allington and P. H. Johnston, eds., *Reading to Learn: Lessons from Exemplary Fourth-Grade Classrooms,* pp. 140–165. New York: Guilford.

Johnston, P. H., T. Bennett, and J. Cronin. 2002b. "Literate Achievements in Fourth Grade." In R. L. Allington and P. H. Johnston, eds., *Reading to Learn: Lessons from Exemplary Fourth-Grade Classrooms,* pp. 188–203. New York: Guilford.

Johnston, P. H., H. W. Jiron, and J. P. Day. 2001. "Teaching and Learning Literate Epistemologies." *Journal of Educational Psychology* 93, 1: 223–233.

Johnston, P. H., and M. E. Quinlan. 2002. "A Caring, Responsible Learning Community." In R. L. Allington and P. H. Johnston, eds., *Reading to Learn: Lessons from Exemplary Fourth-Grade Classrooms,* pp. 123–139. New York: Guilford.

Johnston, P. H., and P. N. Winograd. 1985. "Passive Failure in Reading." *Journal of Reading Behavior* 17, 4: 279–301.

Kameenui, E. J. 1995. "Direct Instruction Reading as Contronym and Eonomine." *Reading and Writing Quarterly: Overcoming Learning Disabilities* 11: 3–17.

Kingsolver, Barbara. 1989. "Quality Time." In B. Kingsolver, ed., *Homeland and Other Stories.* New York: HarperCollins.

Kondo, D. K. 1990. *Crafting Selves: Power, Gender, and Discourses of Identity in a Japanese Workplace.* Chicago: University of Chicago Press.

Kuhn, D., M. Garcia-Mila, A. Zohar, and C. Anderson. 1995. *Strategies of Knowledge Acquisition* 60, 4. Chicago: Society for Research in Child Development.

Ladson-Billings, G. 1994. *The Dreamkeepers: Successful Teachers of African American Children.* San Francisco: Jossey-Bass.

Langenhove, L. v., and R. Harre. 1999. "Introducing Positioning Theory." In R. Harre and L. v. Langenhove, eds., *Positioning Theory: Moral Contexts of Intentional Action,* pp. 14–31. Oxford: Blackwell.

Licht, B. 1993. "Achievement-Related Belief in Children with Learning Disabilities: Impact on Motivation and Strategy Learning." In L. J. Meltzer, ed., *Strategy Assessment and Instruction for Students with Learning Disabilities,* pp. 247–270. Austin, TX: Pro-Ed.

Lindfors, J. W. 1999. *Children's Inquiry: Using Language to Make Sense of the World.* New York: Teachers College Press.

Lloyd, C. V. 1998. "Adolescent Girls: Constructing and Doing Literacy, Constructing and Doing Gender." *Reading Research Quarterly* 33, 1: 129–136.

Luria, A. R. 1973. Trans. B. Haigh. *The Working Brain: An Introduction to Neuropsychology.* New York: Basic Books.

Lyons, C. 1991. "Helping a Learning Disabled Child Enter the Literate World." In D. DeFord, C. Lyons, and G. S. Pinnell, eds., *Bridges to Literacy: Learning from Reading Recovery,* pp. 205–216. Portsmouth, NH: Heinemann.

Lyons, N. 1990. "Dilemmas of Knowing: Ethical and Epistemological Dimensions of Teachers' Work and Development." *Harvard Educational Review* 60: 159–180.

Lyons, C. A., G. S. Pinnell, and D. E. DeFord. 1993. *Partners in Learning: Teachers and Children in Reading Recovery.* In D. Strickland and C. Genishi, eds., *Language and Literacy* Series. New York: Teachers College Press.

McQueen, H., and I. Wedde, eds. 1985. *The Penguin Book of New Zealand Verse.* Auckland, New Zealand.

Mercer, N. 2000. *Words and Minds: How We Use Language to Think Together.* London: Routledge.

Michaels, S. 1986. "Narrative Presentations: An Oral Preparation for Literacy with First Grade." In J. Cook-Gumperz, ed., *The Social Construction of Literacy,* pp. 94–116. New York: Cambridge University Press.

Miller, D. 2002a. *Happy Reading!* Tape 1: Essentials: Tone, Structure, and Routines for Creating and Sustaining a Learning Community. Portland, ME: Stenhouse. Videotape.

———. 2002b. *Happy Reading!* Tape 3: Wise Choices. Independence and Instruction in Book Choice. Portland, ME: Stenhouse. Videotape.

Miller, M. 1986. "Learning How to Contradict and Still Pursue a Common End—The Ontogenesis of Moral Argumentation." In J. Cook-Gumperz et al., ed., *Children's Worlds and Children's Language.* Berlin: Mouton de Gruyter.

Miller, P. J. 1994. "Narrative Practices: Their Role in Socialization and Self-Construction." In U. Neisser and R. Fivush, eds., *The Remembering Self: Construction and Accuracy in the Self-Narrative*, pp. 158–179. Cambridge: Cambridge University Press.

Mishler, E. G. 1999. *Storylines: Craftartists' Narratives of Identity.* Cambridge: Harvard University Press.

Mitchell, R. W. 2001. "Americans' Talk to Dogs: Similarities and Differences with Talk to Infants." *Research on Language and Social Interaction* 34, 2: 183–210.

Neisser, U. 1976. *Cognition and Reality: Principles and Implications of Cognitive Psychology.* San Francisco: W. H. Freeman.

Nicholls, J. G. 1989. *The Competitive Ethos and Democratic Education.* Cambridge: Harvard University Press.

Niemi, P., and E. Poskiparta. 2002. "Shadows over Phonological Awareness Training: Resistant Learners and Dissipating Gains." In E. Hjelmquist and C. v. Euler, eds., *Dyslexia and Literacy.* London: Whurr Publishers.

Nolen-Hoeksema, S., J. S. Girus, and M. E. P. Seligman. 1986. "Learned Helplessness in Children: A Longitudinal Study of Depression, Achievement, and Explanatory Style." *Journal of Personality and Social Psychology* 51: 435–442.

Nowicki, S., and K. A. Schneewind. 1982. "Relation of Family Climate Variables to Locus of Control in German and American Students." *Journal of Genetic Psychology* 141: 277–286.

Nystrand, M., A. Gamoran, R. Kachur, and C. Prendergast. 1997. *Opening Dialogue: Understanding the Dynamics of Language and Learning in the English Classroom.* New York: Teachers College Press.

O'Reilley, M. R. 1993. *The Peaceable Classroom.* Portsmouth, NH: Heinemann-Boynton/Cook.

Palmer, P. J. 1993. *To Know as We Are Known: Education as a Spiritual Journey.* San Francisco: HarperCollins.

Pintrich, P. R., and P. C. Blumenfeld. 1985. "Classroom Experience and Children's Self-Perceptions of Ability, Effort, and Conduct." *Journal of Educational Psychology* 77, 6: 646–657.

Pontecorvo, C., and L. Sterponi. 2002. "Learning to Argue and Reason Through Discourse in Educational Settings." In G. Wells and G. Claxton, eds., *Learning for Life in the 21st Century: Sociocultural Perspectives on the Future of Education*, pp. 127–140. Oxford: Blackwell.

Poskiparta, E., P. Niemi, J. Lepola, A. Ahtola, and P. Laine. 2003. "Motivational-Emotional Vulnerability and Difficulties in Learning to Read and Spell." *British Journal of Educational Psychology: British Psychological Society.*

Pradl, G. M. 1996. "Reading and Democracy: The Enduring Influence of Louise Rosenblatt." *The New Advocate* 9, 1: 9–22.

Pressley, M., R. L. Allington, R. Wharton-MacDonald, C. Collins-Block, and L. Morrow. 2001. *Learning to Read: Lessons from Exemplary First-Grade Classrooms.* New York: Guilford.

Pressley, M., S. E. Dolezal, L. M. Raphael, L. Mohan, A. D. Roehrig, and K. Bogner. 2003. *Motivating Primary Grade Students.* New York: Guilford.

Pressley, M., and V. Woloshyn. 1995. *Cognitive Strategy Instruction That Really Improves Children's Academic Performance*, 2nd ed. Cambridge: Brookline Books.

Randall, W. L. 1995. *The Stories We Are*. Toronto: University of Toronto Press.

Ray, K. W. 1999. *Wondrous Words. Writers and Writing in the Elementary Classroom*. Urbana, IL: National Council of Teachers of English.

Reichenbach, R. 1998. "The Postmodern Self and the Problem of Developing a Democratic Mind." *Theory and Research in Social Education* 26, 2: 226–237.

Repacholi, B. M. 1998. "Infant's Use of Attentional Cues to Identify the Referent of Another Person's Emotional Expression." *Developmental Psychology* 34: 1017–1025.

Riessman, C. K. 1993. *Narrative Analysis*. Vol. 30. Newbury Park, CA: Sage.

Rio, P. d., and A. Alvarez. 2002. "From Activity to Directivity: The Question of Involvement in Education." In G. Wells and G. Claxton, eds., *Learning for Life in the 21st Century: Sociocultural Perspectives on the Future of Education*, pp. 59–83. Oxford: Blackwell.

Roeser, R., C. Midgley, and T. C. Urdan. 1996. "Perceptions of the School Psychological Environment and Early Adolescents' Psychological and Behavioral Functioning in School: The Mediating Role of Goals and Belonging." *Journal of Educational Psychology* 88: 408–422.

Rogoff, B., and C. Toma. 1997. "Shared Thinking: Community and Institutional Variations." *Discourse Processes* 471–497.

Schaffer, H. R. 1996. "Joint Involvement Episodes as Context for Development." In H. Daniels, ed., *An Introduction to Vygotsky*, pp. 251–280. London: Routledge.

Schunk, D. H., and P. D. Cox. 1986. "Strategy Training and Attributional Feedback with Learning-Disabled Students." *Journal of Educational Psychology* 78: 201–209.

Scollon, R. 2001. *Mediated Discourse: The Nexus of Practice*. New York: Routledge.

Scollon, R., and S. Scollon. 1981. *Narrative, Literacy, and Face in Interethnic Communication*. Northwood, NJ: Ablex.

Seligman, M. E. P. 1975. *Helplessness: On Depression, Development, and Death*. San Francisco: W. H. Freeman.

Senge, P. M. 1994. *The Fifth Discipline: The Art and Practice of the Learning Organization*. New York, Doubleday.

Skinner, E. A., M. J. Zimmer-Gembeck, and J. P. Connell. 1998. Individual Differences and the Development of Perceived Control (#254). Monographs of the Society for Research in Child Development, 63, 2–3: 220.

Steig, W. 1976. *The Amazing Bone*. New York: Puffin Books.

Sutton-Smith, B. 1995. "Radicalizing Childhood: The Multivocal Mind." In H. McEwan and K. Egan, eds., *Narrative in Teaching, Learning, and Research*, pp. 69–90. New York: Teachers College Press.

Taylor, B. M., D. S. Peterson, P. D. Pearson, and M. Rodriguez. 2002. "Looking Inside Classrooms: Reflecting on the 'How' as Well as the 'What' in Effective Reading Instruction." *The Reading Teacher* 56: 70–79.

Tomasello, M., and M. J. Farrar. 1986. "Joint Attention and Early Language." *Child Development* 57: 1454–1463.

Vygotsky, L. S. 1978. *Mind in Society: The Development of Higher Psychological Processes.* Cambridge: Harvard University Press.

———. 1986. *Thought and Language.* Cambridge: MIT Press.

Wagner, B. M., and D. A. Phillips. 1992. "Beyond Beliefs: Parent and Child Behaviors and Children's Perceived Academic Competence." *Child Development* 63: 1380–1391.

Wegerif, R., and N. Mercer. 1997. "Using Computer-Based Text Analysis to Integrate Qualitative and Quantitative Methods in Research on Collaborative Learning." *Language and Education* 11, 4: 271–286.

Wells, G. 1998. *Dialogue and the Development of the Agentive Individual: An Educational Perspective.* Aarhus, Denmark: ISCRAT98. http://www.oise.utoronto.ca/~gwells/Iscrat.agentive.txt accessed 2/15/04.

———. 2001. "The Case for Dialogic Inquiry." In G. Wells, ed., *Action, Talk and Text: Learning and Teaching Through Inquiry,* pp. 171–194. New York: Teachers College Press.

Wentzel, K. R. 1997. "Student Motivation in Middle School: The Role of Perceived Pedagogical Caring." *Journal of Educational Psychology* 89: 411–419.

Wertsch, J. V., P. Tulviste, and F. Hagstrom. 1993. "A Sociocultural Approach to Agency." In E. A. Foorman, N. Minick, and C. A. Stone, eds., *Contexts for Learning: Sociocultural Dynamics in Children's Development,* pp. 336–356. New York: Oxford University Press.

Wharton-McDonald, R., K. Boothroyd, and P. H. Johnston. 1999. Students' Talk About Readers and Writers, Reading and Writing. Paper presented at the American Educational Research Association, Montreal.

Wharton-McDonald, R., and J. Williamson. 2002. "Focus on the Real and Make Sure It Connects to Kids' Lives." In R. L. Allington and P. H. Johnston, eds., *Reading to Learn: Lessons from Exemplary Fourth-Grade Classrooms,* pp. 78–98. New York: Guilford.

Wood, L. A., and R. O. Kroger. 2000. *Doing Discourse Analysis: Methods for Studying Action in Talk and Text.* Thousand Oaks, CA: Sage.

Wortham, S. 2001. "Narratives in Action: A Strategy for Research and Analysis." In A. Ivey, ed., *Counseling and Development Series.* New York: Teachers College Press.

Young, R. 1992. *Critical Theory and Classroom Talk.* Philadelphia: Multilingual Matters.

Also Available from Stenhouse

Reading with Meaning
Teaching Comprehension in the Primary Grades

Debbie Miller

Imagine a primary-grade classroom where all the children are engaged and motivated; where the buzz of excited, emerging readers fills the air; where simultaneously words are sounded out and connections are made between the books of their choice and the experiences of their lives. Then, open these pages.

Welcome to Debbie Miller's real classroom where real students are learning to love to read, to write, and are together creating a collaborative and caring environment. In this book, Debbie focuses on how best to teach children strategies for comprehending text. She leads the reader through the course of a year showing how her students learn to become thoughtful, independent, and strategic readers. Through explicit instruction, modeling, classroom discussion, and, most important, by gradually releasing responsibility to her students, Debbie provides a model for creating a climate and culture of thinking and learning. You will learn:

- techniques for modeling thinking;
- specific examples of modeled strategy lessons for inferring, asking questions, making connections, determining importance in text, creating mental images, and synthesizing information;
- how to help children make their thinking visible through oral, written, artistic, and dramatic responses to literature;
- how to successfully develop book clubs as a way for children to share their thinking.

Reading with Meaning shows you how to bring your imagined classroom to life. You will emerge with new tools for teaching comprehension strategies and a firm appreciation that a rigorous classroom can also be nurturing and joyful.

2002 • 208 PP/PAPER • COLOR INSERT • 1-57110-307-4

Also Available from Stenhouse

Happy Reading!
Creating a Predictable Structure for Joyful Teaching and Learning

Debbie Miller

How does Debbie create a learning environment that fosters such sophisticated talk around texts? How is comprehension instruction balanced with teaching decoding skills? How does she help students develop the skills in independence and collaboration necessary for successful reading workshops? Debbie and her students tell this story through a wealth of classroom segments as Debbie reflects on the reasoning behind her instructional decisions and the connections between her practice and the theories that inform her work.

While many examples of Debbie teaching comprehension and students practicing reading strategies are presented, they are only part of a larger portrait of how she carefully organizes the classroom environment and designs effective instruction. You will see her assessing students in the midst of teaching, tailoring instruction to emerging needs, and taking the time to build a community of learners.

Tape 1: Essentials: Tone, Structure, and Routines for Creating and Sustaining a Learning Community
This tape documents how and why the room is organized to support readers; the basic components of readers' workshop; how to get started with students who have few decoding skills; and the rules and procedures for whole-group sharing, conferences, and small-group work.

Tape 2: Explicit Teaching: Portraits from Readers' Workshop
This tape presents explicit teaching in a variety of contexts, including: word study; scaffolding individual readers in conferences; using observations to assess students; whole- and small-group instruction in comprehension; and small-group guided practice in decoding.

Tape 3: Wise Choices: Independence and Instruction in Book Choice
Informed student book choice is essential to a successful reading workshop. Students need a balanced reading diet of different types of text, and when we teach them how to make good choices it fosters independence and engages and motivates them to read for longer periods of time. Nonfiction is key, and teaching students how to access it broadens their choices and helps them become successful in a variety of texts with varying degrees of difficulty.

2002 • 3 30-MINUTE 1/2″ VHS VIDEOTAPES + VIEWING GUIDE •
1-57110-357-0 • NOT AVAILABLE FOR RENTAL